the Zinester's Guide to Port[land]

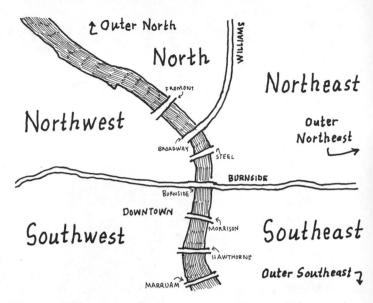

How to Use this Guide

We broke the *Zinester's Guide to Portland* into sections to make it easy to find what you need. There are separate sections by type of business. Reference the section for the kind of establishment that you are looking for with categories such as "Restaurants," "Theaters," and "Parks." Reference the location of where you are and where you are headed to make sure there isn't a similar type of place in walking distance and figure out how to reach your destination! If you are looking for something specific, look for it in the Index at the back of the *Guide*.

Things change; use the phone numbers and/or websites provided to check that a business is open.

And just because a business is mentioned in the *Guide*, it doesn't mean that the authors are 100% behind it; ownership or quality of services can change. Take all listings with a grain of salt and rely on your own judgement.

If you find errors or omissions, please contact us:

PDXGuide.org • 2752 N Williams Ave. Portland, OR 97227

CONTENTS BY: Shawn Granton (unless otherwise specified)
BOOK DESIGN: Joe Biel • **FACT CHECKING & PROOFREADING BY:** Tomy Huynh

COVER BY Shawn Granton; INTERIOR ART BY: Nate Beaty (nb), Shawn Granton (sg), Lydia Greer (lg), Chris Larson (cl), Alec Longstreth (al), Carolyn Main (cm), Dan Miller (dm), Bruce Orr (bo), Heather Q (hq), Khris Soden (ks), Eliza Strack (es), Dylan Williams (dw)

Thank you to all of those who have helped out by contributing writing, art, or something else to the *Zinester's Guide* over the past fifteen years: Nate Beaty, Elijah Brubaker, Jessica Byers, Joe Biel, Chris Cilla, Ezra Claytan Daniels, Krissy Durden, Nicole Georges, Rebecca Gilbert, Uriah Herr, Alicia Justus, Scott Larkin, Kate Lopresti, Seann McKeel, Greg Means, Jay Moreno, Emily Nilsson, Aaron Renier, Androo Robinson, Nickey Robo, Tim Root, Rio M. Safari, RevPhil Sano, OBE., Molly Springlmeyer, Eliza Starky, Ian Stude, Jon Van Oast, Alex Wrekk, and Eleanor Whitney, who put together the first edition in 2001.

Introduction

Welcome to the newest and latest edition of the *Zinester's Guide to Portland*! Thank you for playing. We've been doing this guide since 2001, when it was simply a small, hastily gathered handout for the first Portland Zine Symposium. Over the years, and with the help of dozens, we have the larger and hopefully more informative guide you see here!

The question that I've asked myself when preparing this edition is: Is the *Zinester's Guide* still relevant? First off, we always assumed "zinedom" to be a fairly homogenous body, y'know, cheap, vegan, punk rock. Of course, that's not really the case, but the guide was informed by those sensibilities. So we still skew towards low-to-no cost things to do, restaurants that have plentiful vegetarian/vegan options, and things like that.

But in this age of smartphones, Google, and Yelp, is a humble printed guide still relevant? Well, let's just say that the paperback version of this guide was always far more popular than its website counterpart, so much so that we've taken that down to focus on the book. While you can simply go on Google Maps, type in "coffee shops," and get scads of listings, how do you know that they're good? Well, hopefully the reviews will tell you something. But this method of searching gets cumbersome pretty quickly. And do you know who these people reviewing stuff are? Well, yeah, you can check their profiles and all, but…that's even more work!

What we hope to cover in this guide are some of the things in town we feel are worth checking out, for the most part. These are places we've been to, and would recommend to someone if they're looking for a park, or for a place for a cup of coffee, to get some good food, and to pick up a zine! (People still make them.) We're not that interested in the "hottest" places, or places you have to wait in line for an hour, or places that just make you feel not worthy of being there, or places that make you feel bad in general.

Portland is changing. Many feel that the rate of change is a bit too much to handle. And a bound and printed document in this digital age is going to have limitations. Things close down. Places begin to suck. So take what we say with a grain of salt. Also, we decided to not include hours of operation in this guide. For one, these things can change too often, and we'd rather not have you get mad that the record store was closed even though we said it should be open! And in this age of smartphones and Google, it's pretty easy to check open hours. We've provided phone numbers when we know them, so even if you have an old flip phone, you could still make a call to find out.

And please remember, we can't be all things to all people. We aren't going to include every coffee shop in Portland; that would be too much! We just want to give you a good representation of what's good and worthwhile here. Feel free to explore and try other places that are not listed. And sorry that we didn't include your business in here. Maybe you opened right before we got this to print, we don't know about you, or we ran out of room. Please don't take it as a slight.

Hope you enjoy! And explore Portland.

SHAWN GRANTON
"EDITOR"

A note about the illustrations within:

Everything pictured in this guide is a hand-drawn illustration. Not many guides feature actual illustrations in the way we use them. Our artists spent a lot of time drawing these pieces.

If your business is depicted in an illustration in the *Zinester's Guide to Portland*, please note that every illustration is copyrighted by its respective artist. If you would like to use that illustration, please contact us first. We'll put you in touch with the respective artist and they can give their approval. And hey, if you are a business, give the artist something for their work. It may not have to be actual money, it could just be free tickets to a movie, some coffee, a gift certificate, services that you offer, etc. In short, be nice about it and please don't use a drawing without checking first.

A Brief History of the City of Roses

BY KHRIS SODEN

In 1841, near the beginning of the great overland migrations to the Oregon Territory, two men sharing a canoe ride from Fort Vancouver (in what is now Washington State) to Oregon City stopped in a low clearing to rest during the afternoon. One of the men, William Overton, a drifter from Tennessee, stated that the area was his land claim, and that if the other man, Asa Lovejoy, a lawyer from Boston, would pay to file the land claim, Overton would give him half-ownership. Lovejoy liked the location, and agreed to do it. Several months later, Overton sold his half of the claim to Francis Pettygrove, a merchant from Maine, for fifty dollars in supplies, and then left the area, never to be heard from again. Lovejoy and Pettygrove started clearing trees in the area, platting roads, and laying the groundwork for a new townsite. Unable to agree on a name for their future city (they both wanted to name it after their hometowns), they agreed to flip a coin on it. Pettygrove won, and named the fledgling town site Portland in honor of Portland, Maine.

In 1851, when the settlement had grown to a population of 850, Portland was officially incorporated as a city. During this time, Portland enjoyed considerable economic growth as the Northwest's only shipping port (Seattle had yet to be founded), and was doing brisk business with San Francisco, thanks to California's gold rush. Sea trade was also being done with the East Coast, the Sandwich Islands (now Hawaii), and China. This trade, along with the eventual depletion of gold in California, brought an influx of immigrants to Portland, and the city had grown to a population of 70,000 by the beginning of the 1880s.

Like all cities, Portland developed its own personality, and in the case of the City of Roses, it was a split personality. On its most public face, Portland was a gentile, blue-blooded community; on the other side was Mr. Hyde: a city of racism, vice, and corruption. This was perhaps most evident in the 1880s when Portland was investing in education and city parks, and gaining a reputation for being the "roughest seaport in the World." Portland purchased the first city block for the Park Blocks in 1867 and in the 1880s acquired City Park (now Washington Park). Public schools had been in place for nearly twenty years, and a public library was in the works. Steven Skidmore bequeathed a public fountain to be built in the commercial center of the city. During this period, there was a backlash against the Chinese population, which comprised nearly a third of the city's citizens. Riots against the Chinese led to an exodus of sorts, with many of them returning to China or relocating to San Francisco. The need for able-bodied seamen prompted the practice of "shanghai-ing," or kidnapping men to sell to unscrupulous captains in need of crew. The North End (now known as Old Town/Chinatown) was a haven for prostitution and drugs, much as it is today. Police corruption was rampant, and the entire force was replaced twice during the 1880s.

By the turn of the century, Portland attained the status of a small metropolis. To prove it, in 1905, the city hosted a World's Fair-style Lewis and Clark Centennial Exposition. Built around the now-filled-in Guilds Lake in Northwest Portland, the Exposition featured cultures from around the world, extravagant electric lighting, and the world's largest log cabin (which later housed the World Forestry Center until the structure burned down in 1964). Over one-million people visited the Exposition that summer, and many moved to Portland afterwards. By the 1920s, Portland's population exceeded 250,000. The early part of the century also brought progressive politics and planning to the city's government.

During World War II, Portland was one of the primary centers for ship building. By the end of the war, roughly 150,000 people were employed by the shipyards, with a large percentage of them being African-Americans who had come from the East for work. Predominantly white Portland showed its racist stripes when mortgage insurance companies "red-lined" black neighborhoods to imply they were bad risks. In 1950, an anti-discrimination ordinance was defeated in the general election.

Through the late 1950s and 1960s, Portland embarked on ambitious series of "urban renewal" projects, the first (and probably the most devastating) being the South Auditorium Urban Renewal Project, which almost entirely erased South Portland, displacing thousands of the city's Jewish and Italian families. The Stadium Freeway project destroyed fourteen city blocks of downtown, and the Fremont Bridge sliced through Albina. The Morrison Bridge eradicated seven blocks of downtown's original Chinatown.

Although the city had done a good deal of damage to its cultural and social aspects during the middle of the twentieth century, the 1970s saw the beginning of a new era for Portland, when the city began to refocus on neighborhoods, parks, and public transportation. Through public protest, a plan to cut the Mount Hood Freeway through the middle of Southeast Portland was scrapped, and on the edge of the Willamette, Waterfront Park was created on the site of the former Harbor Drive highway. In 1979, the Urban Growth Boundary was established to combat the sprawl that had affected other Western cities. Light rail (MAX) came to the city in 1986.

Today, Portland likes to endorse its livability and the "creative class" of citizens, such as artists, musicians, and designers. Unfortunately, an aspect of promoting these is the gentrification of older neighborhoods and higher rental rates. The city has become more careful about preserving its historic past and architecture, but it sometimes still turns a blind eye to "developing" neighborhoods.

It's a great city to ride a bike in. At least, if you don't mind a little rain.

Portland's Transit System

The Portland area has a healthy mix of transportation options, especially for a mid-sized American city. Most (if not all) of a visitor's, or a Portland resident's, transit needs is provided by one agency: The Tri-County Metropolitan Transportation District of Oregon. Thankfully it's commonly known as TriMet, so you don't have to memorize that mouthful. TriMet covers all of the city of Portland and its suburbs within Multnomah, Clackamas, and Washington counties. There are other transit agencies, which service distant towns, that connect to TriMet, but within the metro area TriMet is what you'll use. (The one big exception is C-Tran, the system that services Vancouver and Clark County, Washington, which you would use if you cross the Columbia.)

TriMet operates five light rail lines (in order based on when they were opened: Blue, Red, Yellow, Green, and Orange), one commuter rail line (Westside Express Service or WES), two modern streetcar lines (under contract to the city of Portland), and, the backbone of the system, 80 bus lines. Service is provided from about 5 am to 2 am each day (unfortunately there is no overnight/"night owl" transit service.)

Overall, TriMet is a decent public transportation system, especially for a city of our size. It's not as big and extensive as the ones in New York, Chicago, or Los Angeles (and let's not compare it to European or Japanese cities.) Sadly, it's not as good as it used to be. Gone are the days of Fareless Square, the free transit zone in the central city. Also gone are the magical paper transfers that might last for hours and hours. Now they've been replaced with a date-stamped automated ticket good for exactly two-and-a-half hours. (It used to be only two hours, so that's an improvement.) Service cuts over the years have dropped some routes and curtailed service on others, while the price of a basic fare keeps on going up. (I've seen the base fare increase 100% in the fourteen years that I have lived here, from a base rate of $1.25 in 2001 to $2.50 in 2015.) And TriMet consistently fails whenever we get the rare severe winter weather every five years or so, (or for that matter, any sort of unusual weather event) despite promising "it'll be better the next time." But TriMet can still get you to most of the places you need to go. The bus drivers and other transit operators are generally pleasant, professional, and helpful. And unlike other American cities where only the desperate, destitute, or DUI'd use the bus, here you'll find people from all walks of life happily—and willfully—taking transit.

Getting Info

By far, the easiest spot to get the info you need is TriMet's website: trimet. org. While there, you can use the trip-planner tool to route out your journey, check on the status of busses and rails via Transit Tracker, and purchase passes by mail. Contact them by phone at 503-238-RIDE (7433) where you can get automated information 24/7 (and live help if need be on a weekday.) You can also call this number from your bus/rail stop and use the Stop ID number listed at the station to get arrival times via Transit Tracker. (You can do this without a Stop ID, but it'll take longer and only give the arrival info for the nearest major stop to your location.) If you have the Stop ID, you can text 27299 with the number and you'll get a text back with arrival times!

For smartphones and other internet-connected mobile devices, the mobile friendly website is: m.trimet.org. TriMet has its own app available for Android/Google or Apple called "TriMet Tickets" which not only gives you trip-planning tools, but also allows you to purchase either two-and-a-half hour tickets or day passes. Simply activate the "ticket" and show it to the bus driver or Fare Inspector. (The app is OK, but for basic info I prefer either "The Transit App" or "Moovit", both of which show arrivals on nearby transit lines in real time, and also have info for many other cities throughout North America and Europe.)

If you prefer to get your info the old fashioned way/in person, go to the Ticket Office at Pioneer Courthouse Square (701 SW 6th Ave.), which is open 8:30 AM to 5:30 PM weekdays. You can get all the info you need there, pick up paper schedules for all routes or purchase a book that has all the route info, and buy any type of ticket or pass TriMet offers. You can also purchase tickets and passes at the "Neighborhood Ticket Outlets" of Fred Meyer, Safeway, and Albertsons stores in the Portland metro area.

Fares, Transfers, and Passes

The fare structure is pretty simple, as there is only one standard fare: the 2 1/2-Hour Ticket. For $2.50 you can go anywhere in the TriMet system (bus or rail). The fare is good for two-and-a-half hours from purchase or validation time. This ticket is also good as a transfer to another bus or rail line in the TriMet system during this two-and-a-half-hour window. When you board a new bus, simply show your ticket to the bus driver, or to a Fare Inspector on the rail line (if you're asked.)

For $5.00 you can purchase a 1-Day Pass good throughout the system from whenever you purchase or validate the pass until the end of service day. 2 1/2-Hour Tickets and 1-Day Passes can be purchased on the bus, MAX, WES, and Streetcar. (Exact change needed for the bus; ticket machines at rail stops can give change, though it will be in coins.)

TriMet also provides 7-Day, 14-Day, 30-Day, and Calendar Month Passes. You can purchase any of these passes at the Ticket Office at Pioneer Courthouse Square or through the TriMet website. Ticket machines at MAX and WES stations also sell all of the aforementioned passe, while the

Neighborhood Ticket Outlets sell the Calendar Month passes (in addition to 2 1/2-Hour Tickets and 1-Day Passes.) To confuse you even more, the ticket machines at Streetcar stations only sell 2 1/2-Hour Tickets, 1-Day Passes, and special Streetcar Only fares; more about that in a bit.)

The Transit Mall

Running the length of NW/SW 5th and 6th Avenues, between Union Station in the north and Portland State University (PSU) in the south, is Portland's Transit Mall, formerly known as the bus mall. Many bus routes run along the Mall, including the Yellow, Orange, and Green MAX lines, while the Red and Blue lines cross it at Pioneer Courthouse Square. The Transit Mall is the hub of TriMet's system and depending on where you're going. you may have to transfer buses (or trains) here.

MAX Light Rail

First opened in 1986, the MAX (Metropolitain Area Express), has grown into a fairly extensive rail network of five lines that reaches out to the edges of the metro area. The MAX has won many awards, and after a few trips on it you can see why. While the MAX is not the first modern light rail system in North America (that honor goes to Edmonton, Alberta), it's the first to introduce low-floor cars in 1998, which means no steps to walk up to board. This made it much more convenient for those in wheelchairs or with baby strollers! (And for those of us who bring our bikes along.) Around the same time, the MAX introduced bike hooks, making it easier to use for cyclists since they no longer need to stand awkwardly with their bikes in the middle of the aisles. (Of course, plenty of folks still do that, esp. if the hooks are full.) All cars except the old-style "step-up" cars feature these hooks, allowing the storage of four bikes per car (plus two extra floor spots if not occupied by a wheelchair.) The Red/Airport Line opened in 2001 creating a direct rail link to the airport. With the opening of the Green Line in 2009, Union

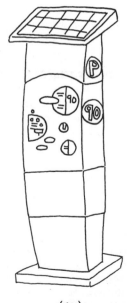

(gm)

Station also has a light-rail link, meaning you can hop off Amtrak (or even Greyhound) and get on light rail!

In my biased opinion, these are the three coolest parts of the MAX system:

- The Steel Bridge: Where all but the Orange Line converge on the upper deck. The lower deck hosts both freight and passenger (Amtrak) rail. Along with cars, buses, pedestrians, and cyclists, this has to be one of the most multi-modal (if not the most multi-modal) bridge in the entire world!
- The Tilikum Crossing Bridge: The brand spanking new rail bridge for the Orange Line. It also gives passage to bicycles, pedestians, buses, and emergency vehicles, but get this, no private motor vehicles are allowed!
- The Robertson Tunnel: A twin-tube tunnel 2.9 miles (4.7 km) long passing through the West Hills (Tualatin Mountains.) This allows MAX access to the westside suburbs. There's one station in the tunnel, the Washington Park/Oregon Zoo stop, which at 259 feet (79 m) deep is the deepest subway station in the United States and the fifth deepest in the world. This is cool enough by itself, but since "ground level" at the entrance to the station is nearly at the top of the hills, cyclists can get a li'l downhill action. It only took four years from the opening of the station in 1998 for some enterprising folks to create a whole new bike culture tradition out of this known as Zoobomb. More about that later!

WES Commuter Rail

WES (Westside Express Service) is the Portland area's only "traditional" commuter rail, meaning actual railroad cars on actual railroad tracks. The tracks here are owned by Portland and Western Railway, which also operates the trains (modern rail deisel cars now known as muliple deisel units) under contract to TriMet. The line opened in February of 2009 and provides service between Beaverton and Wilsonville on the west side of the metro area. Unlike some other commuter rail systems that only provide inbound service during the AM rush hour, and then outbound service during the PM (cough cough, Seattle, cough), trains operate in both directions during the service day. The service day is not long, though: Trains run about every half hour weekdays from roughly 5:15 AM to 9:30 AM, and then again from 3:30 pm to 7:30 pm. There is no service on weekends. Just like other TriMet rail vehicles, you can bring your bike on board. In the years since WES has been in operation, I've yet to take a ride on it, though I've promised myself I will some day! Unless you're doing commuting along the Hwy. 217 corridor in Washington County, I doubt you'll be riding WES.

The MAX! (nb)

Portland Streetcar

Entering service in 2001, the Portland Streetcar is the nation's first "modern" streetcar system. Unlike most light rail systems, which either operate on their exclusive right-of-way or segregated from other traffic when on city streets, the Portland Streetcar primarily operates on city streets mixed with regular traffic, just like old streetcar systems. Unlike MAX, which often uses two-car trains, all of the Streetcars are single cars with a low floor area in the center of the car for easy boarding/unboarding. The system slowly built up over the past fifteen years, and now there's the main loop running downtown (mostly along 10th Ave. and 11th Ave.) and on the eastside via Martin Luther King Jr. Blvd. and Grand Ave. (The loop is completed at the Broadway and Tilikum bridges.) There's also a spur into NW Portland (the original line.) So it breaks down into three distinct lines:

- The North/South (NS) Line: a 4-mile (7-km) line from Legacy Good Samaritan Hospital (NW 23rd Ave) via NW Lovejoy/ Northrup, and NW/SW 10th and 11th Aves to the South Waterfront District.
- The A Loop: a line that operates clockwise along the loop route.
- The B Loop: a line that operates counter-clockwise along the loop route.

You can use the same fares on the Streetcar that you use with any other TriMet vehichle. However, there is a "Streetcar Only" fare of $2.00 available only at streetcar stops that is good for two-and-a-half hours. The main complaint levied against the Streetcar is: "I can walk faster than it!" So then, why don't you just walk?

Portland Aerial Tram

Opened in late 2006, this aerial tramway is the second of its kind in the U.S., after the Roosevelt Island Tramway in New York City. It carries people between South Waterfront district and the main Oregon Health & Science University (OHSU) campus up on Marquam Hill. The tram travels a horizontal distance of 3,300 feet (1,000 m) and a vertical distance of 500 feet (150 m). Cool, huh? The round-trip fare (they don't sell one-way tickets) for the Tram is $4.50, but they only check if you are going up to Marquam Hill, so if you are going down, free ride! (You can take the 8 bus up to OHSU.) The Tram operates on weekdays from 5:30 AM to 9:30 PM, Saturdays from 9 AM to 5 PM, and Sundays only during summer. (It's also closed on major holidays.) The Tram is as much of a tourist draw as it's a commuter vehicle since you can get an expansive view of the city and the mountains on the three-minute ride.

The Bus

Yep, you know what it is! There are 80 distinct bus lines serving the metro region. All buses have bike racks that can hold two bikes, and most buses are of the "low-floor" variety. Unlike other major cities, all of our buses are "standard" sizes, which means they're about 30- to 40-feet long (no double-long articulated buses to be found here). In addition, 13 of the 80 routes are "Frequent Service" lines, meaning service every 15 minutes or less during the main part of the day every day. (All MAX lines are also "Frequent Service.")

TriMet! (nb)

The Neighborhood Guide

The city of Portland is divided into five sectors: Northwest, Southwest, Southeast, Northeast, and North. Burnside Street divides north from south (addresses on Burnside are either W or E), and the Willamette River divides east from west. When the city planners were devising this "quadrant" system to compartmentalize Portland in 1931, they noted that the Willamette made a 45° turn just north of the Burnside Bridge. This would have caused some points in the Northeast to be farther west than some points in the Northwest! The compromise was to create a "North quadrant," separate from the Northeast one using Williams Avenue as the divider.

(There's also a more obscure, smaller "compromise" area in SW, since Naito Pkwy. is "zero line" here. Any addresses on west/east streets east of Naito Pkwy. start with zero; so if an address is 0123 SW Curry St., you know it's east of Naito, wheras 123 SW Curry would be west of Naito. Got that?)

All addresses in the City of Portland contain the respective sector they're located in, noted by the abbreviations SE, NE, SW, NE, and N (for example: 2026 NE Alberta St.). A "block" in Portland is 100 street numbers, and there are 20 "blocks" to a mile. Also, west/east streets are labeled "Streets", while north/south streets are "Avenues." In most areas of Portland, the north/south Avenues are numbered. (The big exception to that rule is North Portland, where all Streets and Avenues have names. There are other exceptions scattered throughout the city.) So this makes navigation a piece of cake! If an address is, say, 1201 NE Fremont St., you know it's on an west/east Street, and it's between NE 12th and 13th Avenues. If you had to get from 1201 NE Fremont St. to 3201 NE Fremont St., you know it would be one mile, since 20 blocks equal a mile. And to be even more helpful, newer street signs will also have the block number on them. So 3501 NE Fremont would be on the 3500 block, meaning 35 blocks north of Burnside, or a distance of 1 3/4 miles from Burnside.

In general, when residents are asked where they live, they refer to their sector (for example: "I live in Southeast" or "I live in North Portland"). In each of these sectors, there are a multitude of unique neighborhoods. Here's a brief rundown of Portland's quadrants to help you explore the city more effectively.

Northwest

The Northwest is a divergent mix. While its sections closest to the river are the most densely settled areas in the whole state, it contains Forest Park, a large tract of undeveloped parkland. It's also quite possibly the wealthiest quadrant in the city, with most of it gentrified. There are still bits of the ol' grit to be found, but they're few and far between.

The Northwest Hills is the general term for the north-of-Burnside neighborhoods that straddle the Tualatin Mountains. Here you'll find some great views of the city (especially at Pittock Mansion), and some really nice homes. Downhill, you'll find the "heart" of this sector, the boringly named "Northwest Neighborhood" (more "sophisticated" residents like to refer to it as "Nob Hill"). This neighborhood is bounded by W Burnside, I-405, the Willamette, NW Nicolai, and the Hills. Up until the 1990s, this area was less expensive, more working class, and a bit dodgy (*Drugstore Cowboy* was shot here). However, due to the combination of lots of old apartment buildings (one of the few places in the city to find such a concentration of pre-war apartments), fairly intact commercial streets, and its proximity to downtown, the area started to appeal to young professionals, and it got gentrified.

The dual business axis of this area is NW 21st Ave. and NW 23rd Av. Twenty-Third (sometimes derisively referred to as "Trendy-Third") is a "see-and-be-seen" type of place and really appeals to those who like to shop. All sorts of corporate chain stores can be found here (Pottery Barn, Urban Outfitters, etc.), plus way-overpriced, wait-two-hours-to-be-seated type restaurants, and two Starbucks. There are still some cool things here, but sometimes dealing with the "23rd Attitude" isn't worth it. Twenty-First is more laid back, more bar-and-food and less "boutique." But the frat mentality here is quite high on the weekends.

On the east side of I-405 is the Pearl District (bounded by I-405, W Burnside, NW Broadway, and the river). Until the mid-1990s, this was a forgotten warehouse-and-industrial district, with its streets crisscrossed by railroad tracks. Then, like the rest of Northwest, the Pearl was "discovered." (The moniker "Pearl District" became a thing when gentrification started; up until then, the area was known as the Northwest Industrial District.) Now many of the warehouses are filled with lofts and art galleries. Some would like to consider this the "artistic heart of the city", but no struggling artist would be able to live here these days.

If you go farther east, you'll find Old Town (bounded by NW Broadway, W Burnside, and the river). This is historically Portland's "Skid Row" (along with the Skidmore Historic District just to its south). For now, the area still retains much of its grit, filled with nightclubs that appeal to suburban bros, plus transitional housing. Within Old Town, you'll find our postage-stamp-sized Chinatown.

Southwest

The Southwest quadrant can be divided into three distinct zones. The first zone is the old core of SW. This contains Downtown, which is pretty self-explanatory (tall buildings, businesspeople, offices, city government, stores, and the like). Hugging the Willamette and spreading southward towards the city line are the older urban neighborhoods of South Portland. There are a lot of cool old houses and some sweet views to be found, but getting around the neighborhood is a bit of a clusterfuck, as major highway projects over the years have Balkanized what remains. Seems like you can't go two blocks without having to figure out how to get around another freeway. Along the river is the new South Waterfront District, filled with sparkly glass towers reminiscent of Vancouver, B.C. It's going to take a decade (or two) to see if this area is going to feel like a real place, though.

Traveling west from the core area is the second distinct zone, the Southwest Hills. Here you'll find some splendiferous parks, like Washington Park and Council Crest, awesome views, narrow and windy roads, and tons of spendy houses. This is the area people move to when they "make it", unless they desire the bouregois paradise known as Lake Oswego.

The third zone is, for want of a better term, Outer SW. Before World War II, this rolling landscape was sparsely developed and much of it was not even part of the city. During the postwar boom, the area rapidly suburbanized. Multnomah Village is probably the coolest area out here, as it was developed as a "streetcar suburb" in the early 20th century. Along with the more modern and suburban Hillsdale just to the northwest, you'll find most of the interesting things to do in this part of town. It's an area I like to go check out a few times a year, but it's more designed to be the commercial hub of outer SW than a "destination." There are also some cool parks tucked into the various valleys and hills like Tryon Creek State Park and Gabriel Park. But when you explore outer SW, you definitely feel the "outer," as the area can seem a world away from the rest of Portland.

Southeast

Most of Portland's population lives in the three quadrants on the east side of the Willamette, and it's easy to see why when you look at a map: SE, NE, and N contain most of Portland's area. Southeast is usually people's "first stop" on the Eastside. And to many living here, the Eastside is "where it's at." This wasn't always the line of thinking, and some folks living on the west side still haven't gotten used to it yet.

Southeast is probably the most developed and most "hip" area east of the Willamette. This is probably because of its many distinct neighborhoods and commercial districts, and it was the first area east of the

Northwest/Southwest

Willamette to gentrify. Nowadays it's hard to think of any area of SE, save outer SE, as "gritty," but just 20 years ago many of the areas we now think of as hopelessly gentrified were pretty dam sketchy. For example, SE 34th and Belmont used to be heroin central!

The first neighborhood in Southeast coming from downtown is Buckman (bounded by the river, E Burnside, SE 28th, and SE Hawthorne). The western part of Buckman (up to SE 12th) along with the adjoining areas to the north and south is also referred to as the Central Eastside Industrial District. Lots of warehouses abound here, some of which used to house artists. Many of these folks have been priced out as developers are converting these lofts to condos. Also adding to the area's cool is Lower Burnside, the new nightlife district lining E Burnside from the bridge to 12th. What was once an area known for used car lots, sketchy motels, and street deals is now home to hip and trendy places like Doug Fir and Jupiter Hotel.

East of Buckman is Sunnyside (bounded by SE 28, SE Stark, SE 49th, and SE Hawthorne), originally a "streetcar suburb." Sunnyside is possibly the most "happening" neighborhood in Southeast (though not for long), as it contains both the Belmont and Hawthorne commercial districts. This is the area that many new residents of Portland desire to move to (I can attest to that), but the rents in the area are not cheap.

The Hawthorne district extends primarily from SE 30th Ave. and SE 42nd Ave. along Hawthorne Blvd. (although stuff can be found as far west as SE 11th and as far east as SE 52nd). This area was once a run-down commercial strip, but it has seen quite a transformation over the last decade or so. Now it's the "bohemian" district of PDX. When most mainstream guidebooks used to talk about the Eastside, Hawthorne was usually the only thing mentioned, and described using adjectives such as "quirky" and the ever-stupid "funky." (Now they probably ignore Hawthorne and emphasize Division.) Expect to encounter several shops to buy neat gifts, cheap eats, head shops, cool record and book stores, street musicians, hippies, spangers, and relentless petitioners.

Belmont is Hawthorne's younger cousin, located six blocks north of Hawthorne. Centered on SE 34th and SE Belmont, there's a plethora of good eateries, coffee shops, and markets in a very small area.

South of Buckman is Hosford-Abernathy (bounded by the river, SE Hawthorne, SE 30th, and SE Powell). The two things H-A is most known for is Ladd's Addition and the Clinton St. commercial district. Ladd's Addition is bounded by SE Hawthorne, SE 12th, SE 20th, and SE Division. Ladd's is unique because its streets are laid out in a radial "X" pattern (rather than the grid that the rest of PDX is based on). William Sargent Ladd, a prominent businessman and mayor, subdivided what was his 126-acre farm here in 1891. Inspired by Pierre L'Enfant's plan for Washington, D.C., Ladd designed the plat based on a diagonal street system surrounding a central park

(Ladd Circle). Also included are four diamond-shaped parks, located where some of the diagonal streets meet. Stroll through Ladd's and peep the cool turn-of-the-century arts-and-crafts houses, rose gardens, and stately Dutch elms that line the streets.

The Division-Clinton district is the new "happening" area in SE. While stuff on Clinton St. is centered on SE 26th and SE Clinton, Division's district extends from about SE 20th to Cesar Chavez (39th). Division was fairly sleepy up until five years ago, with some cool things scattered in the mix. Since then there has been an EXPLOSION of construction, making the street unrecognizable from what it was. Lots of four story apartment/condos, each one having ground-floor retail. Lots of hip shops and restaurants name-checked in the *New York Times*. The 180 that was experienced on Division woke up the neighborhood and the rest of city, and now people are on edge regarding all the change going down in Portland.

To the east, you'll find Mount Tabor, the Eastside's highest point and its namesake park. Around this "mountain," there are four neighborhoods that incorporate "Tabor" into their respective names. Mount Tabor (the neighborhood) surrounds Mount Tabor (the "mount") and is mostly residential. South Tabor is, um, south of there, and is also predominately residential. To the north is North Tabor, which has a nice little business district along NE Glisan. And then to the east is Montavilla, a syllabic contraction of Mount Tabor Village. This used to be the end of the Belmont streetcar line, so a business district sprung up around SE Stark and 80th. (There's also a less concentrated business district to the north on NE Glisan.) Montavilla was one of Portland's forgotten neighborhoods, mostly because it was on the "wrong side" of Tabor. Things changed, however, as more people were looking for affordable houses to buy, and realized, "hey, Montavilla ain't so bad after all and it's not as far away as I first thought!" So this means two things: no more cheap housing, and there's finally stuff to do in that forgotten business district!

Sellwood-Moreland, or more popularly just Sellwood, is the southernmost neighborhood along the east bank of the Willamette River and before the city of Milwaukie. Sellwood is one of Portland's most distinct neighborhoods partially due to its distance from downtown, and because it was once a separate city like St. Johns to the north. The neighborhood is also unique in that it has two separate commercial axes, one centered between SE Milwaukie Ave. and Bybee Blvd., and one centered between SE 13th Ave. and Tacoma St. While both areas have become somewhat yuppified, Milwaukie/Bybee stays truer to its roots as Sellwood's "downtown," containing the services the area needs (grocery stores, hardware stores, banks, post offices). Tacoma/13th has become Portland's "Antique Row" and, as such, has assumed the attitude suited to such a district.

Sellwood is a pretty quiet neighborhood, filled with nice houses and big trees. The riverside has been maintained in its natural state for the most part, providing great opportunities to see nature in the city. The bluff above the river bottoms provide choice views of the city, most notably along Sellwood Blvd. and behind Llewellyn School.

To the east of Sellwood are Westmoreland, Reed, and Woodstock. Westmoreland is possibly Southeast's wealthiest neighborhood, filled with big houses. (Our current mayor Charlie Hales happens to live here.) Reed contains Reed College, Portland's most famous/infamous institution of higher learning and unconventional thinking. (Steve Jobs briefly went to school here.) Woodstock is a middle-class 'hood with a distinctive business district along its namesake boulevard. And much to the neighborhood's chagrin, Woodstock contains possibly the largest number of unpaved streets within central Portland.

Heading into deeper Southeast you'll find various neighborhoods clumped around SE Foster Road, one of Portland's few diagonal streets. While we now refer to them using their proper names of Foster-Powell, Mt. Scott-Arleta, Brentwood-Darlington, and Lents, for many years this area was derisively known as Felony Flats. There are definitely bits of that old grime that remains. It's one of the few truly affordable areas in inner Portland that remains, so it's become a destination for first-time homeowners who want to fix up their digs. And while Foster Road hasn't become the "destination" that some (including me) thought it would be by now, there are lots more going on here than in the past. Now the city is committed to making improvements to Foster itself, including bikeways and lowering the speed limit, so it could happen!

Northeast

The Northeast is an interesting mix of different, contrasting neighborhoods. Northeast contains what some used to consider "bad areas," though a lot of those assumptions had to do with poor knowledge of the area mixed with a dash of racism. Over the past decade, those "bad areas" have been heavily gentrified, forcing Portland to have some tough talks about race and class (that is, when Portland wants to have these conversations, which isn't often.) Northeast also contains some of the most affluent neighborhoods in Portland.

The first neighborhood in Northeast from downtown and via Burnside Bridge is Kerns (bounded by the river, I-84, NE 32nd, and E Burnside). Probably due to the proximity of both Sandy and I-84, Kerns is lousy with apartment complexes: some are cool Southern-California-Spanish-Mission-Courtyard style from back in the 20s and 30s, some are ugly 70s shitboxes. A commercial strip along E 28th Ave. between NE Glisan and SE Stark has been revived. This area used to be a "red-light" district up until the

Southeast

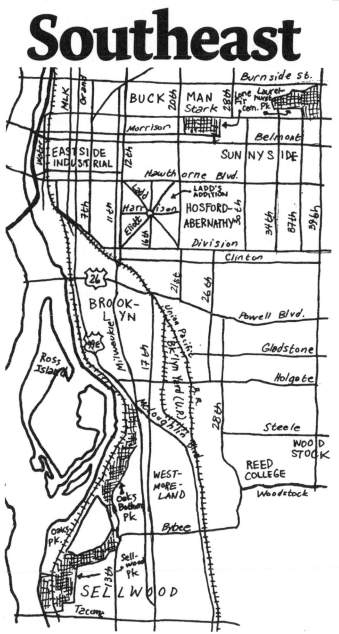

new century, and has since seen an extensive cleanup. Here you'll find wine bars and gourmet eateries sitting side-by-side with some older businesses.

Eastward is Laurelhurst (bounded by NE 32nd, I-84, NE 45th, and SE Stark), a "streetcar suburb." The streets here follow a weird pattern, meandering around the hill rather than following a grid. Laurelhurst was owned by W.S. Ladd, and as with other Ladd properties that have turned into neighborhoods (Ladd's Addition and Eastmoreland), the area is particularly well-off. In the middle is Coe Circle, where NE Cesar Chavez Blvd (39th) intersects NE Glisan St. Check out the gold-leaf statue of Joan of Arc there.

Going north of I-84 closest to the river is the Lloyd District (bounded by the river, I-84, NE Broadway, and NE 16th). This area is the brainchild of a California oil millionaire, who started buying up the land before World War II in order to create an auto-friendly "second downtown" to compete with the first. With its all-too-easy access to the Banfield Expressway (I-84), it became home to Oregon's first enclosed shopping mall, the Lloyd Center. Beside the mall are tall office complexes surrounded and isolated by a sea of parking lots. Well, that's someone's idea of progress, right? Anyways, it's easy to get here via transit, and developers are building lots of apartment buildings now, which hopefully will make this area not feel dead at night. (Don't hold your breath. Those new apartments aren't going to be affordable.)

To the north and east of Lloyd, you'll find Northeast's "money belt." Here's a series of neighborhoods (almost exclusively residential) that are full of spendy, "nice" houses. From west to east, they are Irvington, Alameda, Grant Park, and Beaumont-Wilshire. Through the "money belt" runs the Alameda Ridge, the only significantly steep hill in this part of town. Occasionally, you'll peep a nice view of the city along it, but gargantuan houses have blocked out most of the overlooks, since developers made no provisions to provide any type of parkland along it. It's only by happenstance we have parkland along it east of NE 62nd at Rose City Golf Course. Along the ridge are secret public stairways leading to the streets below (keep your eyes peeled for them!) Also in the area is NE Klickitat Street, famed residence of Beverly Cleary's Ramona the Brave (check out here statue in Grant Park!).

Eastward along infamous Sandy Blvd. is Hollywood (bounded by NE 37th, NE Thompson, NE 47th, and I-84) This was Portland's first "second downtown" (does that make any sense?), predating the Lloyd District by a couple decades. And by "second downtown" I mean a commercial hub far from downtown that provides services for those who didn't want to travel all the way to the city center. Much of this district was built in the 1920s, during the time when streetcars were still dominant but the automobile was coming on strong. Hollywood's sleepy feel has persevered throughout the ages, as suburbia expanded farther out and new auto-dependent

Joan of Arc in Coe Circle, NE Cesar Chavez & Glisan (al)

shopping centers stole Hollywood's thunder. Because of that, you'll find some stuff you won't find elsewhere like a couple of old-school Chinese restaurants, a soda fountain, and the Hollywood Theatre, which is one of the greatest cinemas in the Northwest. Surrounding Hollywood is Rose City Park, a neighborhood possibly containing the city's largest collection of bungalow-style houses.

Heading north is where the current "action" of the Northeast is. North of NE Fremont St., you'll find the neighborhoods of King, Sabin, Vernon, Woodlawn, and Concordia. Formerly a predominately African-American area, these neighborhoods have seen an influx of new ethnic groups into the area. Most conspicuous is the infusion of white twenty-somethings, attracted by affordable housing. Gentrification has been a hot topic as new blood displaces older residents and 'hood stalwarts slowly close, leaving few reminders of what these neighborhoods used to be. The long-established commercial artery is NE Martin Luther King Jr. Blvd. (Oregon Route 99E). The newer commercial strip of this area is Alberta Street (or if you prefer, "Alberta Arts District"), which is the barometer of what's occurring here. The District runs along Alberta St. approximately between NE 12th and NE 31st Aves, cutting through most of the above-mentioned neighborhoods. Once a decimated light-industrial and commercial zone, it's now dominated by art galleries, restaurants, coffee shops, boutiques, and new apartment/condo developments. Alberta hosts the "Last Thursday Artwalk." During the nicer months, Last Thursday is quite the spectacle, packed all the way

Northeast

up-and-down with people displaying their wares on the street, random street theater, and tons and tons of people. Last Thursday has been a point of contention over the last few years, as older residents resent all the attention and the "bridge and tunnel" crowds who flock to it. There's also been heat with the city because of the extra resources needed to deal with it. (They close the street during the nicer months, and that's only happened because an open act of defiance prompted it.)

Going farther east you'll hit up neighborhoods like Roseway and Madison South. These areas are mostly residential, with businesses on the main arteries of Sandy and NE 82nd Ave. Cully is an interesting anomaly, as before the 1990s the neighborhood was outside the city limits, which means it was outside of the city's zoning. The negatives are that it lacks services, most of its streets lack sidewalks (at least, the ones that are paved), and it had lacked municipal sewer lines (homeowners had to shell out big bucks to get their homes upgraded). The positives are the lower housing prices, the abundance of big property lots, and the funky, forgotten, almost rustic feel of

Paul Bunyan statue in Kenton (North Portland) (sg)

the 'hood. It's a neighborhood where you'll see a lot of chicken coops and big gardens.

North

The North "quadrant" was the "secret" part of inner Portland. While not far from downtown, or particularly hard to get to, it was still enough off the beaten path for traditional guidebooks not to have featured it for years, and for most casual visitors to the city not to have visited it. (And even some people who had been living in the city didn't know that there was a "North Portland!") But now, North Portland is on the radar.

Just to note: most residents simply refer to this sector as "North Portland," rather than "the North." Some people call it NoPo, but the real hip kids refer to it as "the Peninsula," since both the Willamette and Columbia rivers form boundaries.

The closest neighborhoods to downtown are Boise and Eliot

North

(collectively bound by the river, N/NE Broadway, NE MLK/7th, NE Skidmore, I-405, and I-5). These districts are also the heart of Albina. After World War II, Albina was the epicenter of African-American Portland. Because of that, Albina used to be synonymous with "ghetto" and "the wrong side of the tracks" for several decades. Albina was a settlement in the mid to late nineteeth century that became its own city in 1887. It was then consolidated with Portland (the original city located on the westside of the Willamette) and East Portland (Albina's east bank neighbor to the south) into one city in the 1890s. Boise/Eliot has two commercial cores: one along N Mississippi Ave., the other along N Vancouver/N Williams Aves. Just like Northeast, there has been a recent influx of new people in the neighborhood. Mississippi rapidly gentrified in the mid-aughts, turning what was a mix of light-industrial and boarded-up storefronts into one of the "hippest" neighborhoods in town. Vancouver and Williams is also seeing an explosion of four-story apartment buildings and fancy new businesses.

Heading westward is Overlook, which straddles the bluff "overlooking" the Willamette. In this primarily residential area, there are plenty of great views of the city and the West Hills (some of which are a bit secret, so get exploring!). N Interstate Ave. is the primary north/south artery here, with businesses lining both sides of the street. TriMet opened Interstate Max (Yellow Line) in 2004, which increased development on the then moribund corridor (Interstate Ave. is 99W, which was the main route into town from Washington State before I-5 opened). However, Interstate is still nothing like Mississippi or Williams/Vancouver. Make sure you check out the classic neon signs on the motels along the strip while you're here!

Going deeper into the peninsula, you'll encounter several residential neighborhoods like Humboldt, Arbor Ridge, University Park, and Portsmouth. North of Alberta St. between I-5 and MLK is Piedmont, a sleepy zone filled with shady, tree-lined streets and gorgeous old homes.

Farther north is Kenton, located north of Lombard St., west of I-5 and east of Chautauqua. Kenton was established as a company town for the meatpacking industry located along the Columbia River and Columbia Slough in the early 1900s. The company ran a streetcar line from the neighborhood down to the waterfront and built many a worker's house. Kenton contains an old "downtown" along N Denver Ave. where it meets N Interstate. Many of the buildings here are built with cinderblock, a rare sight in this city. This sleepy downtown has woken up since the MAX Yellow Line opened, though there's still a good mix of old and new. Don't forget to check out the Paul Bunyan statue at the intersection of N Interstate and N Denver!

At the tip of the Peninsula in North Portland, you'll find St. Johns (no apostrophe needed!). St. Johns was once its own city, competing for predominance over the Willamette with Portland. While it finally succumbed to the ever-expanding City of Roses in 1915, St. Johns retains its sense of "otherness," at once feeling like its own town, yet still being a part of Portland as a whole. The residents of St. Johns are a proud bunch that have been wary of change, though the neighborhood's hard exterior is chipping away as new blood moves in. "Downtown" St. Johns is located along N Lombard where it intersects with N Philadelphia. The area exudes small-town charm. St. Johns contains a healthy ethnic mix not commonly found elsewhere in the city. Many folks wonder if this area will ever truly be "discovered" (and subsequently gentrified), but its isolation from the rest of the city and the loyalty of its residents runs deep.

Outer East

Though within the city limits, Outer East Portland (or just East Portland to some) feels like a separate city altogether. That's because this area east of I-205 that borders Gresham (our eastside suburb) was not part of the city until the 1980's and 1990's. Made up of parts of Southeast and Northeast, Outer East isn't recognized as a "quadrant." Rather, it's a collection of suburbanized neighborhoods and major arterials. Little in this part of town can be considered a destination (save for some parks like Powell Butte), but it's quite possibly the last inexpensive area to live in Portland without leaving the city limits. As such, many folks, including young "pioneering" homebuyers, who've been pushed out of the inner neighborhoods end up here.

It's going to be interesting to see if Outer East will ever be a desirable place to live. Falling short of that, many folks who live out this way feel ignored by city hall, especially when there are so many things that need to be fixed in the area. Some fed-up residents have threatened to pursue plans to separate Outer East from the rest of Portland, while others want the city's charter to be changed so that there's geographic representation on the city council (currently, Portland has an at-large commissioner government).

Portland Weather Primer

So you've probably heard that it "rains a lot" here in Portland. Maybe you've gone and asked the first Portlander you encountered about it. This usually doesn't go well. You may be asked if you're thinking about moving here. If you reply, "yes," be prepared to be told it's a non stop deluge from October 1st through May 1st. What many Portlanders try to do is scare people off. But if you say you're just here to visit, you generally get a more truthful response.

So here I am to give you the "real" answer. Yes, Portland has a wet reputation, and late fall through late spring is considered the rainy season. But what does this mean? And how wet does it get?

It may surprise you that by U.S. city standards, Portland's yearly rain total is pretty middling and lower than many cities in the East (cities not considered "rainy"). Portland's annual rainfall is 36 inches, which is less than that of Atlanta (48 inches), Birmingham, AL (52 inches), Houston (46 inches), Indianapolis (44 inches), and New Haven, CT (47 inches.)

So if we're drier than Indianapolis, why do we have such a rainy rep? It's because it rains often during the rainier months. Portland gets the majority of rain between November and April. During these months, it can pretty much rain daily. We have had stretches of 30 consecutive days of rain, and we have 155 days of measurable precipitation, which is almost half the year!

Whoa, you may say! Thirty consecutive days of rain? One hundred fifty-five days overall? That sucks. Well, it can. But please let me clarify: It generally doesn't rain all day, and when it rains, it isn't hard rain. Granted, every once in awhile we get a day with pissing rain. But it's mostly off-and-on showers or drizzle. Sometimes during our "rain days" we have sun breaks. But usually the wet days are overcast, which helps bolster the Northwest's reputation for brooding depression.

Well, if the winter is so bleak, why stick around? I can only answer for myself. The one big plus is our winters are cool, not really cold. The average high temperature for January is 45°F (7°C) and low is 34°F (1°C). The temperature rarely dips below freezing, and when it does, it's usually overnight. It's pretty rare when the high isn't above freezing (maybe two days a year if we are so lucky). And it's usually less than 30 days in a year that we get freezing temps. The grass stays green all year! Sure, we're no San Diego, but we're no Saint Paul, either!

So now you may ask, does it snow? Yes, but infrequently. We may get one or two dustings a year. Anything "substantial" (and a couple inches is substantial here) is gone in a day. About every five years, we do get a real snow event here, with several inches of snow that may stick around a lot longer. I've seen it happen three times since I've lived here: 2004, 2008–2009, and 2014. When it does snow, even if it's an inch, the city basically grinds to a halt. Roads snarl with sliding vehicles and abandoned cars, TriMet barely functions, and no one expects anyone to go to work. Now you may feel that it's all rather silly, but when was the last time you had a snow day as an adult?

Enough about winter. How about summer? From June through early October, abundant sunshine is the norm. There can be rainfall any time during the summer months, but it's a rarity. We only see 4.5 inches of rain from June through September. In fact, we're considered a warm-summer

Mediterranean climate! And what's even better: we barely have any humidity in the summer! (Unless you're from SoCal, you'll find our summers "humid".)

The most surprising thing about summer here is how warm it gets. The average high in July is 80°F (27°C) and periods of 90°F (32°C) heat are common. This may come as quite a shock to some, especially to our friends in the South, as they assume we're "cooler" because we're north of them. For comparison, the July high in Oakland is 70°F (21°C), Los Angeles 72°F (22°C), San Diego 72°F (22°C), and San Francisco a relatively frigid 64°F (18°C).

So Californians, remember to bring your shorts! For our Eastern friends visiting during the summer months, remember to pack a hoodie or sweater. Because our summers lack humidity, the temps can drop dramatically overnight. The average low temperature for July is 58°F (15°C), a drop of over 20 degrees from the daytime high!

In the end, it all balances out. Having distinct seasons is fun, and the rain is good. If it weren't for our wet winters, we wouldn't have the towering Douglas Firs and the profusion of greenery everywhere. If it weren't for the rain, we'd be just like California. And we wouldn't want that, would we?

Stereotypical Portland Attractions

Get these things out of the way and move on. (Or just avoid them completely.)

One thing that this guide has been about since its inception is positivity. We're not Yelp, so we're not going to waste our time (and yours) writing negative reviews. But as Portland's reputation builds, there becomes a standard "to do" list for visitors. Many items on these lists are overrated. Maybe they were cool at some point, but they've lost their luster over time. Or maybe they were never that great in the first place?

But I know, you've seen the TV shows and websites telling you to hit up some key attractions. So if you don't, you'll be hounded by your friends back home. In light of this, here is our list of some standard Portland attractions (the things you may want to visit once, and just once to say you did). These are places that most of us who live here try to avoid, so we won't feel bad if you decide not to go!

(hq)

Voodoo Doughnuts: In the early days of the guide, we were worried that this "very Portland" doughnut shop wouldn't last the year. Now we're worried that this juggernaut is going to take over the world! Well, maybe they won't take over the world, but they're actively pursuing the franchise angle. And honestly, their donuts are okay, but you can find better elsewhere. But there's that long line! And we know that long lines mean something's worthwhile, right? And it's cool to get on the plane with the pink box, eh? (Pro tip: If you want to avoid the long line at the main location at 22 SW 3rd, hop over to Voodoo II at 1501 NE Davis, where the line ain't that long. That's where the "Portland natives" go!)

Shanghai Tunnels Tour: There are ancient underground tunnels rumored to have been used for kidnapping drunks and forcing them to work on ships, but there is no actual evidence of this. History indicates that these tunnels were actually used to move heavy cargo underneath city streets to avoid street traffic. While the Shanghaiing mythology is likely false, go on the tour if you like ghost stories.

Waiting in line for food: Is the food at Salt & Straw, Pok Pok, Screen Door, or (insert most recent restaurant hyped in the *New York Times*) really that good, or are you just really hungry after waiting two hours for a seat? Or is it possibly a case of confirmation bias? I don't like waiting in lines, do you? Do you really want to spend most of a short visit waiting in line?

Bars in Old Town during the weekend: Are you a bro or do you like bros? If you answer no to both, get the hell out!

Last Thursday on Alberta: Last Thursday has transformed from a cool place to see art and sell your wares to Portland's coolest free monthly party to a place cool for the bridge-and-tunnel crowd. Not so fun fact: There was a shooting on Last Thursday in early 2015. People took selfies at the crime scene and angry suburbanites wondered aloud if they were going to be denied their Salt & Straw ice cream because of it. (I'm not making this up!) If you want to go, go during the off season when the crowds aren't there.

Portland Saturday Market: Yes, it happens on Sunday too (though closed completely in January and February.) Unless you're the type who typically likes to go to conventional, tourist-oriented craft bazaars, there are better ways to spend a visit to Portland. Pro tip: This is a great place to drop the parents off for a few hours.

Mill Ends Park: Yes, it's the smallest city park in the world. It's also in a traffic island on busy Naito Parkway. Get your picture taken there, and then move on to the much larger and more comfortable Waterfront Park.

Outlet Shopping: Yes, I realize people want (no, demand) cheap prices on "brand-name" goods. And Oregon has no sales tax. But odds are if you're the type of person who reads a guide like this, you're probably not the type interested in shopping at the Woodburn Outlets. (By the way, there's no direct bus service from Portland to the Woodburn Outlets.) For "fun" and as part of my paid job, I figured out how one would get to the Outlets by bus. It is possible, if you want to transfer like four times each way and literally spend all day getting there and back. If you are hell-bent on outlet shopping and have no car, head to Troutdale instead. You can basically take the 77 bus the whole fucking way there!

Looking toward Mt. Tabor (dw)

Some other things to get out of the way:

- You'll mispronounce Willamette and will be constantly corrected until you get it right. Or someone snarky will say, "I'm sorry, I don't know where the Wil-la-METTE River is. But I can give you directions to the Wil-AAH-mit River, if you want."
- You'll ask a local if it rains all the time (See our "Portland Weather Primer" section for the answer.)
- You'll ask a local if they've seen *Portlandia*, and if Portland's really like the show. Don't expect to get a correct answer.

Bars
North

The Alibi Tiki Bar *4024 N Interstate Ave. 503-287-5335 AlibiPortland.com* A remaining relic of old Portland with food and a full bar. Lots of mixed drinks, amazing karaoke, and a laid-back attitude. And fun!

The Waypost *3120 N Williams Ave. 503-367-3182 TheWaypost.com* A warm and unpretentious bar, which is a good antidote to what's happening on the rest of Williams. Holdover coffee is available to appease its old customers from its days as a cafe, and now it has a full bar! The Waypost is a great place to socialize and see informal events.

(World Famous) Kenton Club *2025 N Kilpatrick St. 503-285-3718* Almost nightly live music creates an atmosphere for drinking your beer cozily among friends and future friends. Cheap drinks and friendly staff. The club was used in the film *Kansas City Bomber* with Raquel Welch, hence the "world famous" moniker.

Leisure Public House *8002 N Lombard St. 503-289-7606 LeisurePublicHouse.com* Despite the "classy" name, this joint ain't pretentious. Good prices on beers on tap, plus trivia night!

Twilight Room *5242 N Lombard St. 503-283-5091 TheTwilightRoom.com* This old school Portland haunt is cavernous inside. When it's nice out, the patio is the place to be!

Mock Crest Tavern *3435 N Lombard St. 503-283-5014 MockCrest.com* One of North Portland's not-so-best kept secrets! Leave your pretentiousness at the door; this is a homey, old-school neighborhood spot. Good place for live blues.

Barlow Tavern *6008 N Greeley Ave. 503-289-1163 BarlowTavernpdx.com*
Old-school neighborhood haunt with a friendly vibe, decent-but-greasy food, and a good beer selection.

Interurban *4057 N Mississippi Ave. 503- 284-6669 Interurbanpdx.com*
Swanky joint with extensive whiskey selection. Its big selling point is the bar's streetcar theme, with all the cool stuff on display.

Northeast

Beaulahland *118 NE 28th Ave. 503-235-2794 Beulahlandpdx.com*
Friendly neighborhood bar and eatery. Great beer choices, good jukebox, classic pinball machines, and a pool table. And it's three times as large as it was in the 90's!

High Water Mark *6800 NE MLK Blvd. 503-286-6513* A small, friendly, cozy haunt in the Woodlawn neighborhood with booze, food, outdoor seating, and pinball. Feels laid back and under the radar of the busy city.

Sandy Hut *1430 NE Sandy Blvd. 503-235-7972 SandyHut.com* The Sandy Hut, affectionately referred to by desperate singles as the "Handy Slut," is housed in a purple, windowless, triangular building. Denizens tend to be rough-and-tumble, but it's hard to tell if they're actually like that or if these hipsters are just putting on an act because it's cool to go slumming. Greasy-ass food can be found here, as well as an okay brew selection. The Sandy Hut entered cult status when someone there entered the Portland Adult Soap Box Derby with a car that was a striking replica of the building.

Oregon Public House *700 NE Dekum St. 503-828-0884 OregonPublicHouse.com* This may be the only non-profit pub in the known universe! Most of the staff are volunteers, and profits go to charities. So you can do some good by simply drinking a tasty pint. (And they generally have an interesting tap list to choose from!)

Bye and Bye *1011 NE Alberta St. 503-281-0537 TheByeandBye.com*
Popular hipster joint with great drinks and all-vegan food. Sister bar to the Sweet Hereafter in SE.

Moon and Sixpence *2014 NE 42nd Ave. 503-288-7802* Portland's classic old-British-style pub.

Biddy McGraw's *6000 NE Glisan St. 503-233-1178 BiddyMcGraws.com*
Portland's classic Irish pub.

Southeast

Angelo's *4620 SE Hawthorne Blvd. 503-231-0337* Comfortably situated on the outskirts of the sometimes irritating Hawthorne District, Angelo's offers pint specials, free pool, butt-rock jukebox (you know what we mean), pinball, and friendly bartenders. Nate used to ride almost 90 blocks on a regular basis to frequent this bar, sometimes even through blistering summer heat or torrential downpours (and he doesn't even have fenders on his bike!). But he got alcohol poisoning (not from Angelos, from his high school reunion...long story) and now has the straightedge, maybe.

Basement Pub *1028 SE 12th Ave. 503-231-6068 BasementPub.com* A little of everything good you'd want in a bar. Great food deals, and they offer 20 oz pints for the price of 16 oz. ones at Happy Hour. It also hosts trivia night on Sundays at 9:30 PM, which is quite popular. Get there early if you want to participate.

The Vern (a.k.a. Hanigan's) *2622 SE Belmont St. 503-233-7851* Look for the "tavern" sign with the "t" and the "a" burnt out. Though not quite the dive it used to be, it's still comfortably in the dive category: cheap beer, free/$0.25 pool, good jukebox, holes in the bathroom wall...what else could you want?

Sweet Hereafter *3326 SE Belmont St. Hereafterpdx.com* Go-to bar for good vegan (and only) vegan food, and sister bar to the Bye and Bye in NE. Get the actual Sweet Hereafter drink: a heady cocktail served in a big mason jar. You only need two of them to have a good night!

Lutz Tavern *4639 SE Woodstock Blvd. 503-774-0353* Vintage bar in the Woodstock neighborhood. Supposedly, the recent infatuation with Pabst started here!

Spaceroom *4800 SE Hawthorne Blvd. 503-235-6957* A very 50s, outer-space themed place (the type of joint where you get mixed drinks served in glasses larger than your head!). Alas, the old-school sign out front has been replaced with a more modern and boring one.

Apex *1216 SE Division St. 503-273-9227 ApexBar.com* Bicycle-friendly haunt with giant patio and a ridiculous amount of different types of beer on tap. But don't ask to sample anything because they won't oblige.

Beer

A selection of local brewpubs and the like!

For some, a visit to Portland won't be complete without sampling our local craft-brew scene. Like coffee shops and bike shops, every time I turn a corner, I find a new one that's opened! And of course, that's not a bad thing! Head's up: This list is far from comprehensive. If you want to learn more about Portland's beer scene, check out other guides available both online and in print.

Laurelwood Brewery *Main: 5115 NE Sandy Blvd. 503-282-0622; Northwest: 2327 NW Kearney St. 503-228-5553 LaurelwoodBrewing.com* Great award-winning beers like the organic Free-Range Red and, possibly my favorite, Tree Hugger Porter. The NE taproom can be quite crowded (esp. with young children) during happy hour, so plan accordingly. Laurelwood Brewery's ales are available at many pubs throughout town and they also sell 22 oz. (650 ml.) bottles.

Alameda Brewing *4765 NE Fremont St. 503-460-9025 AlamedaBrewing. com* Look for the large copper hop leaf in front of the building. Alameda is famous for its $5 growler fills on Saturday.

Lucky Labrador Brewing Co. *915 SE Hawthorne Blvd. 503-236-3555; 1945 NW Quimby St. 503-517-4352; 7675 SW Capitol Hwy. 503-244-2537; 1700 N Killingsworth St. 503-505-9511 LuckyLab.com* The Lucky Lab is known for its solid and dependable brews, and for its dog-friendly original location on Hawthorne. The Hawthorne spot is pretty cavernous; it gets loud when there are crowds (it's often crowded!) My favorite spot is the North location on Killingsworth: it's a bit more mellow, they serve pizza by the slice, and you may get served by a former zinester!

New Old Lompoc Tavern and Breweries *Lompoc Tavern: 1620 NW 23rd Ave. 503-894-9374; 5th Quadrant: 3901 N Williams Ave. # B 503-288-3996; Hedge House: 3412 SE Division St. 503-235-2215; Oaks Bottom Public House: 1621 SE Bybee Blvd. 503-232-1728 LompocBrewing.com* Lompoc's specialty is the LSD (Lompoc Special Draft), a nice and hearty ale. My favorite location is the Hedge House, which happens to be a small house surrounded by hedges! (Oh yeah, it has a great patio too.)

Tugboat Brewery *711 SW Ankeny St. 503-226-2508* Tugboat really isn't much of a brewery since it's been brewing the same four beers since I've been coming here. On top of that, it's been out of at least one of its own brews the last few times I've been here. To say that it doesn't care about being the bestest, most exciting brewpub in town is a bit of an understatement.

Thankfully, Tugboat has a good selection of guest taps. And its big selling point is its intimate, hole-in-the-wall setting in the heart of downtown. It's a cozy and warm spot, and I spent a good amount of time here when the IPRC was just blocks away. It also has their share of live music, and is possibly the best spot to see free/experimental jazz in town.

Hopworks Urban Brewery (HUB) *2944 SE Powell Blvd. 503-232-4677; BikeBar 3947 N Williams Ave. 503-287-6258 hopworksbeer.com* HUB was the most talked about brewpub of 2008, and was the winner of the "Most Unlikely Location for a Brewpub" award (lowly Powell Blvd.). The buzz was there for almost a year beforehand due to the fact that the HUB is owned by the former Laurelwood brewmaster. And all of HUB's beers are 100% organic! It specializes in beers on the hoppy end of things. And even though the space feels as big as an aircraft hanger, it can be quite packed, so expect a wait (and a pager like you're at TGI-Fridays or something). The better bet is to hit up smaller BikeBar. Sit out front at this location and watch the bike commuters zip up N Williams. (You can also watch children clumsily attempt to ride the stationary bikes by the front foor, despite signs saying they are not allowed to do so.)

Base Camp Brewing *930 SE Oak St. 503-477-7479 BaseCampBrewingCo. com* One of the newer brewpubs specializing in lagers instead of the typical ales. To get an idea of what it does, try its hoppy India Pale Lager. It also brews some excellent ales like the S'more Stout. Beer to-go is available in traditional six-pack cans or a unique 22-ounce can that's shaped like a bottle! Base Camp's outdoor patio is a great place to hang out on a summer night. Food can be ordered from the two food carts in front of the brewpub.

Ground Breaker Brewing *2030 SE 7th Ave. 503-928-4195 GroundBreakerBrewing.com* Formerly known as Harvester, this brewery and restaurant is 100% gluten free! And yes, its beers are very yummy. So if you had to give up regular beer because of gluten intolerance, check this place out!

Gigantic Brewing *5224 SE 26th Ave. 503-208-3416 GiganticBrewing.com* This gem is tucked into an unassuming corner of industrial SE just north of the Crystal Springs Rhododendron Garden. Gigantic Brewing makes a mighty fine IPA and other good beers. The indoor space is tiny, so the patio is where it's at. And the food truck next door makes one of my favorite veggie burgers!

Montavilla Brew Works *7805 SE Stark St. 503-954-3440 MontavillaBrew. com* This brand new brewpub follows the model I like seeing: small, homey, cozy, humble, and filled with great beers. You probably won't run into the suburban crowd here, but instead friendly neighborhood locals. No food service, but you can bring in your own food.

Sasquatch Brewing *6440 SW Capitol Hwy. 503-402-1999 SasquatchBrewery.com* One of the few brewpubs in the beer wilderness of outer SW. This quaint spot serves as a good gathering spot for the hood, and it has tasty beer to match!

Occidental Brewing *6635 N Baltimore Ave. 503-719-7102 OccidentalBrewing.com* Located in an industrial space practically under the St. Johns Bridge, Occidental specializes in German-style lagers and ales, served in a half-litre glass. No food service, but you can bring in your own food.

Belmont Station *4500 SE Stark St. 503-232-8538 Belmont-Station.com* Belmont Station is a store that regularly features 1,000 different types of beer from every corner of the world! And attached to it is a bier café that features unique, obscure beers on tap. There's also a large patio in the back that's enclosed in the winter. And you can drink any of the 1,000 different types of beer in the bier café if you want (for an additional fee). And don't let the name confuse you, it's *not* on Belmont! (But it used to be.)

Bicycling in Portland

Without a doubt, Portland is a great place to bicycle in. Bike lanes are abundant, the city government actually cares about the plight of cyclists, and motorists tend to be more aware and less antagonistic than in other places. Obviously things are far from perfect, and to some, Portland has recently been lagging behind. Hopefully, things are on the up and up again.

Probably the best way to gauge an area's bikeyness is by counting the number of people you see bicycling. And Stumptown's streets are filled with them! Whether it be the spandex-clad "top-o-the-line" scorcher preparing for her next race, the bike messenger type riding a single-speed with a tiny U-Lock in his back pocket, mommas on giant cargo bikes with three kids in tow, the crazed clowns riding fluorescent-colored choppers, or just an ordinary-dressin' person on a 3-speed with baskets laden with groceries. You'll find every type of bicycle and bicycle rider here.

Portland was made for bicycling. Our winters are relatively mild, so riding year-round is possible. (Of course, you'll have to deal with the rains. Get the appropriate rain gear and you'll cope.) Most places in the central city can be easily reached within a half-hour bike ride. Streets here generally have low-to-moderate traffic amounts, and the six-lane-plus mega-boulevards found in many western cities are far and few between (mostly found in the suburban hinterlands). While not "flat as a pancake" like the

Windy City, major hills are rare here (the notable exceptions being the West Hills, the short-yet-steep Alameda Ridge, the bluffs lining the river in North Portland, and the buttes that pepper the East Portland landscape), so don't expect to encounter the constant ups and downs that are prevalent in Seattle and San Francisco.

Riding a bicycle is, in my humble opinion, the best way to explore this city. While TriMet is reliable and extensive, it doesn't offer the same flexibility you get with a bike. Walking is great and PDX is a pedestrian-friendly city, but the bicycle gives you extended range. And a bike can get to places

(nb)

that a car can never like trails and secret wooded spots. Having a bike allows you to explore every durn neighborhood in this burg, and you'll have the urge to seek out more. So find yourself a bike—whether it be a cruiser, 3-speed, BMX, road bike, mountain bike, fat bike, hybrid, unicycle, etc.—and hit the streets of the Rose City!

Bicycle Shops

Bike Farm *1810 NE 1st Ave. 971-533-7428 BikeFarm.org* Volunteer-run collective that helps you learn how to fix your bike (affordably, too). Check their calendar for women's and trans night.

City Bikes

Main shop: 1914 SE Ankeny St. 503-239-0553; Annex: 734 SE Ankeny St. 503-239-6951 CityBikes.coop This worker-owned cooperative has two convenient locations on Ankeny. The main shop specializes in bike repair and used parts, while the Annex specializes in used bike sales (which they overhaul on-premises) and bicycle accessories. Staff is helpful and knowledgeable. Make sure you schedule an appointment for bicycle work sooner rather than later, since they tend to get quite backed up, especially in summer.

Community Cycling Center *1700 NE Alberta St. 503-287-8756 CommunityCyclingCenter.org* Friendly and inexpensive place to buy used bicycles, and used and new bike parts. Bikestands, tools, and bike-maintenance advice available for free, as well as inexpensive fixes by the volunteers and workers. Many opportunities to volunteer at this community oriented, non-profit shop. Also offers bicycle repair classes.

Recumbent PDX *2025 SE Hawthorne Blvd. 503-231-1000 Recumbentpdx. com* Formerly known as Coventry Cycle Works, this cozy neighborhood shop specializes in, you guessed it, recumbent bicycles (and tricycles!), including sales and service. Regular bikes are serviced too, though recumbents take priority.

Joe Bike *2039 SE Cesar Chavez Ave. 503-954-2039 Joe-Bike.com* Cargo bikes and commuters on the bike highway!

Missing Link Bicycle Shop *7215 NE Sandy Blvd. 503-740-3539; 4635 SE Woodstock Blvd. 503-206-8854 MissingLink.org* This neighborhood bicycle shop once operated out of a van that could make housecalls. Missing Link offers a full line of services and accessories, as well as used bikes for sale. Check out the vintage mid-century American cruisers on display.

North Portland Bike Works *3978 N Mississippi Ave. 503-287-1098 NorthPortlandBikeWorks.org* A non-profit bicycle shop specializing in affordable used and new bicycles, new supplies, and service for the neighborhood. Many programs are available, and there are many opportunities to volunteer and earn credit. Community night occurs once a month when space can be used for free. Women's only night (trans-friendly) is every Wednesday.

PSU Bike Hub *1818 SW 6th Ave. 503-725-9006 pdx.edu/BikeHub/home* The PSU Bike Co-op (now PSU Bike Hub) is a super-cool campus bike shop servicing the Portland State University community. Students, faculty, staff, and alumni are all invited to become members for a per-term or annual membership fee. Members are allowed to use the space and tools during regular hours, get bicycle repair assistance and training from co-op staff, purchase parts and merchandise at a special discounted rate, enroll in Bike Hub-sponsored workshops, and utilize the covered and gated bike parking facility during daytime hours. Not a member of the PSU Community? No worries! You can still buy goods, and get your bike serviced and attend workshops for a small fee. The Bike Hub also rents bicycles and U-Locks.

Sellwood Cycle Repair *7953 SE 13th Ave. 503-233-9392 SellwoodCycle. com* New and used bike sales and service. This place is one of the better ones in town to buy a good used bike. The shop is a big proponent of the local cyclocross scene.

Seven Corners Cycle and Fitness *3218 SE 21st Ave. 503-230-0317 7-corners.com* Friendly shop offering bicycle sales and service.

Weir's Cyclery *5279 N Lombard St. 503-283-3883* Weir's is Portland's oldest bicycle shop (since 1925!) and was owned the Weir family until 2013, when it was sold to Don Richards. The shop has moved around a few times over the last decade (the original shop was just down the street at 5036 N Lombard). It's your typical neighborhood shop, offering bike sales and service.

Velo Cult *1969 NE 42nd Ave. 503-922-2012 VeloCult.com* Velo Cult shook up the bike shop scene when it moved here from San Diego in 2012. Instead of just being a standard bike shop, Velo Cult also decided to open a bar in its cavernous space. It's also an event space that hosts a number of shows and talks throughout the year. In fact, I can almost guarantee you that if there's an event remotely bike related, it's going to be at Velo Cult! Bike nerds beware: The collection of vintage bikes, especially vintage mountain bikes, in the shop will keep you occupied for hours!

Upcycles *909 NE Dekum St. 503-388-0305 Upcyclespdx.com* This friendly li'l bike shop has quite possibly managed to be in every retail space on Dekum between Madrona and Woodlawn Park since its opening in 2010! Its newest and largest space offers a tea house, so you can enjoy a nice warm beverage while your bike gets worked on.

A Better Cycle *2324 SE Division St. 503-265 8595 ABetterCycle.blogspot. com* A worker-owned shop that sells and services new and used bikes, and provides a large selection of used parts as well. Its mechanics are willing and able to work on things other shops don't like to do (or won't do anymore) like cottered cranksets. It's quite possibly the best shop in town for servicing old 3-speeds.

Block Bikes *7238 N Burlington Ave. 503-819-6839 BlockBikespdx.com* Full-service bike shop serving the St. Johns neighborhood, right at the foot of the St. Johns Bridge.

Abraham Fixes Bikes *3508 N Williams Ave. 503-281-6394 AbrahamFixesBikes.com* Small, full-service shop that works on all types of bikes. Abraham also provides the excellent resource *OregonBikeTouring.com* for those of us who like getting out there on our bike for a night or longer.

Clever Cycles *900 SE Hawthorne Blvd. 503-334-1560 CleverCycles.com*
Since its opening, Clever has promoted transportation, utility, and family cycling in Portland. It introduced to town such exotic yet practical bikes like the Bakfiets, a front-loaded cargo bike that holds the kids and/or other cargo, the Brompton, a UK made folding bike, and traditional Dutch city bikes. It offers a wide range of other bikes, accessories, and clothing (stuff that you might not find at other shops). Its mechanics work on all sorts of bikes, but specialize in installing dynamo-powered lighting.

Splendid Cycles *407 SE Ivon St 503-954-2620 SplendidCycles.com* Great shop specializing in all sorts of cargo bikes and electric-assist bikes.

WTF Bikes *3117 SE Milwaukie Ave. 503-232-4983 WTFbikes.net* Yeah, I know what you're thinking, but the acronym actually stands for Well Tuned Fast. Small neighborhood shop featuring full-service sales and repair.

Cat Six Cycles *4831 NE 42nd Ave. 503-282-1178 CatSixCycles.com* Cute li'l shop with full-service repair and new bike sales. Workers can give you a free "Craigslist Consultation" to help you search for a decent bike off ye old CL. Plus, Cat Six features an informal "Open Shop Night" on the first Thursday of the month when you can show up and have access to the shop's tools and knowledge. (Food and drink bribes encouraged!)

21st Avenue Bicycles *916 NW 21st Ave. 503-222-2851 21stBikes.com* This shop took over the former Northwest Bicycles (possibly my fave "old curmudgeon" shop in town). 21st Ave. specializes in urban, touring, and road bicycles.

Fat Tire Farm *2714 NW Thurman St. 503-222-3276 FatTireFarm.com* Portland's long-running mountain bike shop.

Kenton Cycle Repair *2020 N McClellan St. 503-208-3446 KentonCyclepdx. com* Small shop specializing in touring and vintage bikes.

Oregon Bike Shop *418 SE 81st Ave. 503-575-1804 OregonBikeShop.com* Cozy li'l Montavilla stalwart offering new and used bikes, plus full services. Jim and Sue are great folks!

The Outer Rim Bicycle Shop *10625 NE Halsey St. 503-278-3235 OuterRimBicycles.com* Despite Portland being a "bike town", there are only two options in town east of I-205, corporate Performance and local Outer Rim. Located in the Gateway Area, this full-service shop fills the void created when Gateway Bicycles closed. They specialize in BMX, mountain bikes, and cruisers.

Metropolis Bike Repair *2249 N Williams Ave. 503-287-7116 MetropolisCycles.com* Full-service bike shop along the Williams "bicycle superhighway," specializing in wheel building. Also features dynamo lighting.

Backpedal Cycleworks *7126 SE Harold St. 503-891-9842 BackPedalCycleworks.blogspot.com* Neighborhood shop featuring a good selection of used bikes and parts.

Gladys Bikes *2905 NE Alberta St. 503-373-8388 GladysBikes.com* Portland's women-focus bike shop! Gladys' wants to help women fall in love with their bikes, and bicycling in general, by not only offering a space where women can openly talk and ask questions about their cycling needs, but also by stocking lots of products geared towards women. (And don't worry, men, it's perfectly okay to shop here too!) It also offers full-service repair, bike fitting services, and classes. And the shop has a Saddle Library! Have you never found the "right" saddle for you? Are you interested in something like a *Brooks* but don't want to spend the $$ only to find out you don't like it? For a nominal fee you can get a "saddle library card" and try out any of the saddles in the library for a full week! Why hadn't anyone thought of this before?

Bike Rentals and Bike Tours

Pedal Bike Tours *133 SW 2nd Ave. 503-243-2453 pedalbiketours.com* Pedal features bike rentals and a regular offering of local tours. It's also a full-service bike shop.

Cycle Portland Bike Tours *117 NW 2nd Ave 503-739-2453 PortlandBicycleTours.com* Great prices on bike rentals and regular bike tours. And it's a full-service bike shop to boot!

Waterfront Bikes *10 SW Ash St. #100 503-227-1719 WaterfrontBikes. com* Longtime shop featuring bike rentals and sales.

Everybody's Bike Rentals and Tours *305 NE Wygant St. 503-358-0152 pdxbikerentals.com* Everybody's specializes in refurbished road, mountain, and single-speed rentals, plus tours. It's encouraged you call or email the shop first, since it has limited hours.

Bike-Related Shops, but not "Bike Shops"

Rivelo *401 SE Caruthers St. Suite 103 971-266-3551 Rivelopdx.com* This new shop is the local outpost for Rivendell Bicycle Works, that iconic Bay Area bike company founded by former Bridgestone USA dude Grant Petersen, though it's much more than that! Yes, you can find some of Rivendell's classic steel bicycles and other Riv. goods, but proprietor (and former Riv. General Manager) John Bennett carries some unique, hard-to-find bike (and non-bike) items. Also, Rivelo has a good stock of Bob Dylan on vinyl.

Sugar Wheel Works *3808 N Williams Ave. #134 503-236-8511 SugarWheelWorks.com* Sugar builds custom wheels (and damn good ones.) That's it.

Black Star Bags *2033 SE Hawthorne Blvd. 503-284-4752 BlackStarBags. com* Since 2006, Black Star has been making custom messenger bags, backpacks, panniers, and other quality bicycle bags.

North St. Bags *2716 SE 23rd Ave. 503-419-6230 NorthStBags.com* North St. specializes in convertible backpacks/panniers. While other convertibles feature some janky mounting systems and/or things you have to add/remove to make it "work," everything in its convertible backpack/pannier is self contained. North St also makes bike duffel bags, standard panniers, and other bike bags.

Bike Maps

You can find various free, city bike maps directly from the Portland Office of Transportation during normal business hours at 1120 SW Fifth (in the Portland Building), Room 800. Otherwise, these free maps can be found in many bike shops throughout town.

The "Bike There" map is produced by Metro. This big map is water/tear resistant and covers the entire metro area! This map is not free (currently $6), but is well worth the cost, especially if you are going to be doing any longer rides in the area. You can purchase this map at local bike shops.

The State of Oregon produces the Oregon Bicycle Guide (state bike map) and the Oregon Coast bike guide, both free. You may find them at some bike shops, or you can order them directly by emailing MC-RECP: odot@odot.state.or.us

Regular Bikey Events

There could never be a comprehensive list of bicycle events in and around Portland. There are simply too many of them, so we've concentrated on regular alt-bike culture. For more in-depth and up-to-date listings, go to *calendar.ShiftToBikes.org* (the Shift calendar).

EVERY SUNDAY, 8 PM: Zoobomb. Meets at 8 – 9 PM. See Zoobomb listing in the next section for more info.

2nd TUESDAY, 6:15 – 8 PM: Volunteer Night at North Portland Bike Works at 3978 N Mississippi Ave. Learn bike-repair skills, and earn volunteer credit hours.

EVERY WEDNESDAY, 6:15 – 8 PM: Women's Bike Repair Night at North Portland Bike Works at 3978 N Mississippi Ave. Free workshops open to all who identify as women (trans friendly). Learn about bike repair on your own bike! (One specific project recommended.)

EVERY THURSDAY, 7 PM: Thursday Night Ride. Meets at Salmon Street Fountain. This ride has been going strong since 2015, becoming the regular social ride in town. Basically, it's a big bike party, with a bunch of people riding together around town.

2nd FRIDAY: Do you like riding your bike at night? Do you like to ride with a group of folks? Do you like surprises thrown into the mix? If so, check out the Midnight Mystery Ride. Meet up for this event occurs at a local bar between 11 PM and midnight. At the stroke of 12, the ride departs. But where does it go? A-ha, only the ride leader knows! The group traverses the city streets for 1 to 5 miles, and ends up at a secret location. Check out *MidnightMysteryRide.wordpress.com* for the meeting location of the upcoming ride, and also to learn how you, yes YOU, can lead your own ride!

LAST FRIDAY, 7 – 9 AM: Do you bicycle commute to work, and don't have the time to eat or, gasp, have coffee on the way? Don't fear, brave bicyclist, help is on the way! Breakfast on the Bridges provides free coffee, pastries, and other snacks to those riding to downtown from the eastside. Stop a couple minutes, chat with fellow bicyclists, and refresh. Oh, and don't worry about being late to work! Breakfast on the Bridges has regularly occured on the Hawthorne Bridge since its inception. In 2015 it can also be found on the Burnside, Steel, and Tilikum Bridges. (Tilikum may be on a different date.) To learn more, or to volunteer, email timolandia@gmail.com or check the Shift calendar.

JUNE: Pedalpalooza. Portland's annual celebration of bikey fun! Basically a continuation of Bikesummer 2002, this is a three-plus week celebration of bicycles, with events coming in from different sources. This festival regularly features 300 different bike events! For more info, go to *ShiftToBikes.org.*

JUNE: World Naked Bike Ride. An annual event that takes place on a Saturday night. Tens of thousands dress as bare as they dare and take to the streets to demonstrate the vulnerability of cycling in the city, as well as the city's overall fun-loving, quirky nature. Pro tip: They don't publish the route in advance. Don't be a gawker; be a participant! Info at *WorldNakedBikeRide. org.*

SUMMER/FALL: Disaster Relief Trials. Scads of cargo-bicycle enthusiasts demonstrate how they would move supplies and provide disaster relief in the wake of the impending Cascadia Subduction Zone Earthquake! (It's gonna be the big one.)

SUMMER: Sunday Parkways. Ride your bike or skateboard with 30,000 other smiling people in a 6 to 9 mile car-free loop to see a different neighborhood on Sundays from May through September. A truly magical experience where kids say the darndest things like "Why can't we do this every day?" A fine point. Info at *portlandoregon.gov/transportation/46103*.

Useful Tips and Advice for Bicycling in Portland

Lock your bike! Bike thievery is a big problem here. Even leaving your bike unguarded for "just a sec" could mean it's gone forever. Invest in a good U-Lock! When locking your bike to a rack or pole, make sure you have at least one wheel and a part of the frame inside the lock and secured to the rack. Remove anything from your bike that someone can potentially take— especially lights!

Use lights at night! It's safe and it's the law. Oregon law requires a bicycle must have a white light visible at least 500 feet from the front, and a red light or reflector visible at least 600 feet from the rear. Yeah, you can "cheap out" and get the most basic blinkie, but for just about $30 you can get a very bright LED headlight that's rechargeable via USB.

Watch out for the tracks! PDX has many railroad and streetcar tracks that criss-cross around the town. Stories of unsuspecting bicyclists "biting it" when encountering the rails are heard far too often here. (And I'm a member of the "eating it on the tracks" club.) Don't get hurt and have to go to the hospital! To avoid injury, ALWAYS cross tracks at, or as close to, a right angle as possible. Slow down when crossing. Be especially careful when it's wet out. And know your bike: fatter tires can handle tracks and road imperfections better than thin road tires. Also to note: It's perfectly legal to ride on the left side of a one-way street, so you can avoid the tracks on, say, SW/NW 10th and 11th.

Don't ride on the sidewalks downtown. While it's legal to sidewalk ride in other areas of the city, it's not legal downtown. "Downtown" is roughly defined as the area hemmed in by the Willamette, I-405, and NW Lovejoy St. Cops like to ticket bicyclists on this one, so watch out. And if you do sidewalk ride, please note that by law you cannot travel faster than walking speed on a sidewalk where riding is permitted.

Don't ride in the "bus/transit only" lane in the downtown Transit Mall or any other bus-only lanes. There are combined bus/bike lanes that are OK to ride.

Most of the Willamette River bridges are crossable, except for the Marquam and Fremont (both freeway crossings). The Tilikum only allows bikes and pedestrians (along with transit). The Hawthorne, Morrison, and Broadway have sidewalk bicycle lanes that connect to bicycle routes on either side of the river. The Steel has a walkway on the lower deck that connects the Waterfront Park path (westside) with the Eastbank Esplanade. The Burnside has bike lanes on the bridge, but has poor connections off the bridge. And whenever the new Sellwood Bridge opens, it'll have good bike facilities. While you can legally cross the three other Willamette spans (Sellwood, Ross Island, St. Johns), none of them have good bike facilities.

The two bridges that span over Columbia River into Vancouver, WA are the Interstate (I-5) and the Glenn Jackson (I-205) bridges. Both are crossable by bike, if you get the jonesin' to head for the 'Couv. Tip: It's better to use the Glenn Jackson Bridge southbound, because the northbound trip is long and uphill.

Bicycle Advocacy, Culture, and Fun

Shift Born out of Portland's Bikesummer 2002, Shift is a bicycle advocacy organization that works to promote Portland's creative bike culture and highlight bicycling's positive contributions to the community. It plans, executes, publicizes, and has a hand in an ever-widening variety of bike-related events. There are no membership lists, so you don't have to pay any fees or dues to be a part of it. Their website features an extensive calendar of bike-related events.

Zoobomb Is it a cult? Or a way of life? Whatever it may be, Zoobomb is fun. The deal: Every Sunday night, a gang of bike-folks meets up at "The Pile" at W Burnside and 12th between 8 and 9 PM. At 9, everyone takes their bike (or one of the library bikes provided) to the nearest MAX station to catch a train to the Washington Park/Zoo Station. They ride from the station to the top of the hill, hang out a bit at a "secret" location, and then "bomb" down the steep, winding road through the park back down to the Civic Stadium station, I mean, PGE Park station, I mean Jeld-Wen Field station. This is usually repeated a few times, with refreshing done at the top. Fun! The initiated ride children's bikes (referred to as "little" bikes) with 12 to 20 inch wheels.

(es)

As with many activities in this vein, Zoobomb has felt the heat of, well, "the heat." TriMet fare inspectors have given participants grief (a note to the wise: Always pay the fare if you plan on riding the MAX to Zoobomb, otherwise you might end up with a ticket for fare evasion!), the neighborhood association around the Zoo has been at odds with Zoobomb (going as far as to try to get the MAX station to close early on Sunday nights). Even the Department of Homeland Security has considered it a possible "terrorist threat" at one point!! But those days are mostly in the past, and now Zoobomb is recognized as a "cultural institution."

Cycle Wild This non-profit organization leads several overnight bike-camping trips a year to various destinations. Its website is a good resource for those looking to bike camp or tour, whether locally or farther away. Info at *CycleWild.org*.

Portland Bicycling Facilities

Portland is pretty good when it comes to bike infrastructure. Of course, Portland is nowhere near perfect, and still needs more work. If you subscribe to the *Effective Cycling* philosophy, you'd probably argue against spending money on bike facilities. But here are what we've got:

- Bicycle (multi-use) Paths/Trails: These are bikeways that are totally separated from motorized traffic. These facilities are where you'll see the most "recreational" or weekend bicyclists. There aren't that many in Portland—the longer ones being close to the Willamette (Waterfront Park, Eastbank Esplanade, and OMSI-Springwater) or Columbia (Marine Drive and Columbia Slough) rivers. The longest is the Springwater Corridor in far SE Portland.

Zoobomb (es)

- Bike Lanes: These are the marked lanes on streets, exclusively for bicycle use. Bike lanes are generally found on higher-traffic streets in town. One of the cooler things about bike lanes in town is that some of the "international symbol for bicyclist" painted on certain streets have been altered. Some of them have mohawks, some are reading books, some are playing golf, etc. This has all been done by clever Dept. of Transportation street painters.
- Bicycle Boulevards/Neighborhood Greenways: These are low-traffic through streets designated as bike ways. Many of them feature traffic-calming devices such as street islands and speed bumps, and some of them have special traffic lights to aid bicyclists (and pedestrians) in crossing busy streets. These boulevards are noted by the bike symbol painted onto the streets, and the special signage giving directions and approximate distance to destinations.

Fun Places to Ride Your Bicycle in Portland

Most of Portland is a good place to ride! As long as you avoid some of the busier thoroughfares and know how to get to where you're going effectively (a bike map sure does come in handy!), you'll have fun bicycling around town. There are some areas that are more of a destination for cyclists (especially recreational cyclists) due to either the state of the bicycle facility (bike paths), or because of the scenery. Here are some of popular ones:

The Columbia River and Slough The Columbia Slough area is an interesting mix of riparian forest, marshland, heavy industry, and things that people generally don't want to see (landfills, jails, airports, etc). You could be going by a tranquil pond one minute, and then an auto junkyard the next. The Slough has always been the city of Portland's dumping ground (out of sight, out of mind). That said, there's still some cool nature down here, and bicycling along the slough can be an enjoyable experience. There are several bike paths or lanes paralleling Marine Drive, the major east/west thoroughfare. From NE 33rd Ave. to the I-205 Bridge at 112 Ave., the bike path only crosses a road once, so it's a great place to ride fast and long. And east of there, the bike path is mostly complete all the way to Troutdale, with a few sections of bike lane on Marine Drive. Watch out though, the paths along the Slough provide little in cover, so you'll get baked by the sun in the summer. Right now we don't have one river long or slough long path, though they are getting better connected with each passing year.

The West Hills A great place to ride if you like to get a workout and take in the view of Portland below! Ride up to Council Crest, the highest point in the city at 1070 feet (325 meters) via SW Montgomery Drive. Wind along Skyline Drive, dodging all the fast cars along the way! "Bomb" down Marquam Hill through the OHSU craziness!

Mount Tabor At 650 feet (200 meters), Mount Tabor is one of the highest points on the east side, and a great place to ride. It's also an extinct volcano! Some of the roads on the hill are closed to automotive traffic (all roads are closed to cars on Wednesdays). Huff and puff up to the top and take in the view! Don't get intimidated by all the road bikers beating you to the top!

Laurelhurst, Ladd's Addition, Irvington, Alameda These quiet and quaint neighborhoods on the Eastside, with their upper-income-bracket housing, offer great places to bicycle in peace.

I-205 Bike Path I've watched the I-205 Path turn from a "grit your teeth and get through this" experience into something much more pleasant and easy. The bike path was built along with the freeway in the 1970s: a first for the area. While it was supremely modern for the time, it used to involve several tricky crossings of major streets. But with the building of the parallel MAX Green Line, a lot of improvements have been made. No longer do you have to detour out of your way to cross a street semi-safely since every crossing now uses either a bridge, tunnel, or traffic signal. So you can ride from the I-205 Bridge south to Oregon City (almost) on a low stress corridor. Of course, there's always the omnipresent sound of the freeway...

Gresham-Fairview Trail This three-mile trail connects the Springwater Corrido just east of Linneman Junction in Gresham to NE Halsey St. and 201st in Fairview. In the future, it'll go all the way to Marine Drive!

Trolley Trail This six-mile rail trail starts south of downtown Milwaukie and heads to Gladstone in Clackamas County, just north of Oregon City. As the name implies, this route follows (mostly) a former rail alignment, the Portland Traction Company's interurban line from downtown Portland to Oregon City. (This line merged with what became the Springwater Corridor in Sellwood.) The trail conveniently starts near the south end of the MAX Orange Line. If you need to get to Oregon City by bike (and you should at some point) this is the best way to get there!

Forest Park Most of Forest Park is off-limits to bicyclists, since many trails are narrow, steep, and easily eroded. Besides a couple firelanes, the main place to bicycle is Leif Erickson Drive. This dirt road starts at the end of NW Thurman St. and winds along the hills for 11 miles before terminating at NW Germantown Road, about a mile west of the St. Johns Bridge. The Drive is fairly level, with a few steep hills, but it definitely meanders. It's best suited for wide high-volume tires, but don't let that stop ya. It's a great place to bicycle in the near-wilderness for hours, if you want a different cycling experience!

Willamette Boulevard This street in North Portland begins at N Interstate Ave., one block south of Killingsworth. It cuts westward through residential neighborhoods until it hits Mocks Crest overlooking Swan Island and Mocks Bottom. From there, it follows the bluff, giving great views of the industrial city below and the West Hills across the river. There are bike lanes on Willamette Blvd. between N Portland Blvd. and N Ida St. (at the railroad cut). From there you can continue north to the St. Johns/Cathedral Park neighborhoods. Or use the Peninsula Crossing Trail, a separated path that connects to the Columbia Slough network of trails via the railroad cut.

Banks-Vernonia Trail While this path is quite outside the city, this is a good day trip destination or as part of a longer ride to the coast. It's about 12 miles of quiet farm roads from the end of the MAX Blue Line in Hillsboro to the south trailhead in Banks. From there, this former logging railroad route travels 22 miles to Vernonia. About halfway along the route is Stub Stewart State Park, a great camping destination. On the Vernonia end, there are a couple campgrounds as well. For directions: *PortlandOregon.gov/transportation/article/301633*

Look for these other biking oppotunites in the "Parks" section of guide:
The Springwater Corridor
Eastbank Esplanade
Waterfront Park Path
Willamette River Path
Terwilliger Boulevard
Rocky Butte
Powell Butte

(ar)

Books

ye old Reading Frenzy (nb)

Books, Zines, Comix, & the Like

Editor's Note: It does pain me to do this section. Not because any place below is bad (not ast all), but because in the 15 years of the Zinester's Guide, "editing" this section usually means removing stores that have closed. Thanks, internet!

Bridge City Comics 3725 N Mississippi Ave. 503-282-5484 *BridgeCityComics.com* Sparse and gallery-like comic shop with equal parts mainstream and alternative titles, used and new. Friendly folks at the counter.

Microcosm 2752 N Williams Ave. 503-232-3666 *MicrocosmPublishing. com* Independent publisher Microcosm Publishing, the folks who published this durn book, have a bookstore! Look for the bright orange, no green, shop on N Williams. Everything that Microcosm publishes is here, plus several thousand other titles focusing on self-empowerment, bikes, gifts, and politics.

Reading Frenzy 3628 N Mississippi Ave. 503-274-1449 *ReadingFrenzy.com* The zine mecca of the Pacific Northwest! A great place to browse, purchase, and bump into all those Portland zinesters collecting their consignments. (Yes, Reading Frenzy accepts zines for consignment.) The Frenzy also sells crafty goods and the like from local peeps, and cool stuff from around the world. Readings, signings, and other events occur here throughout the year. Its selection of current alternative and mini comics is hands-down the best in town! No zine-related visit to Portland is complete without visiting Reading Frenzy and the IPRC (Independent Publishing Resource Center).

Black Hat Books *2831 NE Martin Luther King Jr. Blvd.* It lacks posted hours and our efforts to shop here have been unsuccessful so far. But if you make it there and it's open, you're in for a treat. Based on the promises of living legend owner/operator Fred Nemo, this used haunt celebrates shelves as eccentric as African Lesbian separatist fiction. It definitely keeps Portland...Portlandish.

In Other Words *14 NE Killingsworth St. 503-232-6003 InOtherWords. com* Your feminist, non-profit bookstore! In Other Words carries a diverse collection of women's writing. Once a fixture of Hawthorne, it is now located in Northeast with a larger space (and cheaper rent) which will mean a much-expanded selection!

Cosmic Monkey Comics *5335 NE Sandy Blvd. 503-517-9050 cosmicmonkeycomics.com* Cavernous shop offering up mainstream and "alternative" comics, new and used.

Excalibur Comics *2444 SE Hawthorne Blvd. 503-231-7351 ExcaliburComics.net* If the "alternative" comix selection at Reading Frenzy just isn't cutting it for ya, because maybe you want the newest issue of *Green Lantern*, then head here. Excalibur is probably the best (and oldest, opened

(cl)

Powell's (ks)

since 1976) of the traditional comic book stores in town (do those other places still exist?). I mean, c'mon! They've got Howard the Duck pulling a sword out of a stone on their sign. How old school can you get? Pick up your mainstream comix fix, get some backing boards, argue with the counter-jock about the newest Marvel movie, and get in a debate about who would win in a fight: Wolverine or Batman?

Mother Foucault's *523 SE Morrison St. 503-236-2665* Considering that this store is finely curated with used copies of everything from philosophy to literary fiction to poetry to cultural criticism packed onto quaint and well-worn wooden shelves, it's surprisingly not as pretentious as you'd expect. While there's a certain implied intellectualism in, well, a bookstore that specializes in topics like these in a changing industrial neighborhood, this speck is like a window connecting Olde Portland to The Present.

Powell's *Powells.com* The largest independent bookstore in the entire world! No matter how you slice it, it's a booklover's dream, with extensive selections of new and used books. The main store (City of Books) takes up an entire city block (and four floors) and requires a map to navigate it. Loads of author reading type events.

- **Powell's City of Books** 1005 W Burnside St. 503-228-4651 or 800-878-7323 (open even on Xmas!) The big one. The cafe is a good spot to while away a winter's day.
- **Powell's on Hawthorne** 3723 SE Hawthorne Blvd. 503-228-4651 An all-purpose version (albeit smaller) of the main store, divided into three rooms. Also includes the ever-popular Fresh Pot Cafe (see separate listing).
- **Powell's Books for Home and Garden** 3747 SE Hawthorne Blvd. 503-228-4651 Just what the name says! The largest store of its kind in the country. Also connected to Pastaworks.

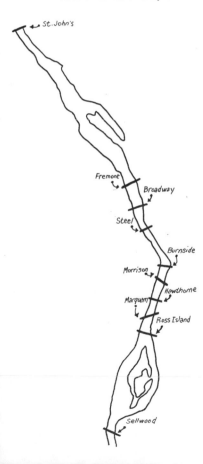

Annie Blooms Books 7834 SW Capitol Hwy. 503-246-0053 AnnieBlooms.com A gem of a bookstore tucked away in cozy Multnomah Village. Annie Bloom's offers a great selection of stuff, including many independently published books. They also host readings and other events regularly.

Floating World Comics 20 NW 5th Ave. Suite 101 503-241-0227 FloatingWorldComics.com Artsy selection of comics, zines, and art books.

Bridges

Here's a quick rundown of info on our beloved Willamette River Bridges, arranged from north to south. For more info, check out the Portland Bridge Book by Sharon Wood Wortman.

St. Johns Bridge US 30 Bypass between St. Johns and Linnton The St. Johns Bridge is one of Portland's most iconic bridges and its only suspension bridge. It's not often seen by the casual visitor (it's about six miles from downtown). Opened in 1931, it was the longest suspension bridge west of Detroit at the time (other bridges have surpassed its length since then, most notably the Golden Gate Bridge). Painted green, the bridge tends to blend in against the West Hills. It's a beautiful bridge and a symbol of pride for the St. Johns neighborhood. The Gothic-arched towers and eastside support beams lends to the name Cathedral Park for the greenspace and neighborhood below.

USAGE: Automotive traffic, pedestrians, and bicycles.

OWNER: State of Oregon.

BICYCLE INFO: You've got two options: ride the sidewalk, or take the lane. When ODOT (Oregon Department of Transportaiton) did work on the bridge in the mid-aughts, they neglected to add bike lanes, which infuriated many a Portland cyclist. The current concession is to put sharrows in the rightmost lanes and put "Bikes on Roadway" signs at each end. Taking the lane on this bridge is not for the faint of heart, despite the fact the bridge is never at capacity. (Hey dude in the big truck, do you really need to buzz me?)

TECHNICAL INFO: Two Gothic towers are 408 ft. tall (124 m), center span is 1207 ft. (368 m), and it's 205 ft. (62 m) above the Willamette River. Total length is 2,067 ft. (630 m).

(nb)

Burlington Northern Railroad Bridge 5.1 (aka St. Johns Railroad Bridge) *On the Willamette River about one mile south of the St. Johns Bridge*
This bridge was built in 1908 to complete the then Northern Pacific (now part of Burlington Northern Santa Fe) mainline north to Seattle. At the time it was a swing bridge, meaning that the center span would "swing" open to

allow for boat traffic. Even though it was the longest swing span in the world, modern maritime needs led to the swing span's obsolescence. In 1989, the bridge was retrofitted with a vertical-lift span. Its twin towers can be seen for miles around.

USAGE: Freight trains (BNSF, UP), and Amtrak.

OWNER: Burlington Northern Santa Fe Railway.

BICYCLE INFO: No bikes!

TECHNICAL INFO: Lift span is 516 ft. (157 m) long, and vertical clearance is 200 ft. (61m). Fourth highest lift bridge in the world.

Fremont Bridge *I-405, between Pearl/Northwest and Albina* Opened in 1973, the Fremont Bridge is the second youngest of Portland's Willamette River crossings. Its beautiful design is due to the Marquam Bridge's (I-5) ugliness—the Portland Art Commission was brought in to aid with the design so there wouldn't be an uproar. (We Portlanders are very particular about our bridges!) Its gentle arch, once the longest tied-arch in the world, dominates the skyline. And peregrine falcons nest on the underside of the span (look closely and you may see one soaring around the bridge!).

USAGE: Automotive traffic.

OWNER: State of Oregon.

BICYCLE INFO: Prohibited! The only legal time you can ride here is during Bridge Pedal in summer.

TECHNICAL INFO: 2,152 ft. (656 m) long, main span is 1,255 ft. (383 m) long, top of arch is 381 ft. (116 m) above the river, and clearance above river is 175 ft. (53 m).

(dm)

Fremont Bridge

D.R.Miller '04

Broadway Bridge *Broadway between NW and N, connects NW Lovejoy and N Interstate* The Broadway is a drawbridge completed in 1913. It's a double-leaf Rall-type bascule bridge, unique in Portland and very rare otherwise. (This bascule bridge is "seesaw" style, with two "draws" lifting up and away from each other to accommodate for riverine traffic) The Rall system uses complicated rolling-lift mechanisms, meaning long delays when the bridge goes up (usually 10-20 minutes).

USAGE: Automotive traffic, Portland Streetcar, pedestrians, and bicycles.

OWNER: Multnomah County.

BICYCLE INFO: Bicycles have bike lanes up until the bridge itself, and then are directed onto the sidewalks. The Broadway is the most popular connection for bicyclists from N/NE to downtown and the Westside.

TECHNICAL INFO: Total length is 1,613 ft. (492m), main span is 278 ft. (85m), and clearance from river is 70 ft. (21m). Painted "Golden Gate" Red (aka International Orange).

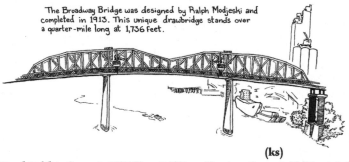

The Broadway Bridge was designed by Ralph Modjeski and completed in 1913. This unique drawbridge stands over a quarter-mile long at 1,736 feet.

(ks)

Steel Bridge *Connects NW Everett/Glisan/Front on the west, N Interstate/ Oregon/Multnomah on the East* The Steel Bridge is a very special bridge. It's the only double-decked vertical-lift bridge with independent lift decks (the lower deck can retract into the upper deck without the upper deck moving) in THE WORLD, and the second-oldest vertical-lift bridge in North America (the first being our own Hawthorne Bridge)! The Steel was built in 1912 by the Union Pacific Railroad, and its primary function was as a railroad bridge, but it's much more than that! It's perhaps the most accomodating and diverse bridge anywhere. Its functionality was increased with the opening of the pedestrian walkway on its lower deck in 2001, completing the downtown waterfront loop. It's quite the experience to ride your bike along the bottom deck while a freight train goes rumbling by! While the Hawthorne is one of Portland's iconic bridges, the Steel is hands-down my favorite.

USAGE: Upper deck: automotive traffic, MAX light rail, TriMet buses, pedestrians, bicycles. Lower deck: freight trains (UP, BNSF, etc), Amtrak, pedestrians, and bicycles.

OWNER: Union Pacific Railroad. Upper deck leased to ODOT and subleased to TriMet.

BICYCLE INFO: The top deck is remedially bikeable, though narrow sidewalks and steep approaches from the west doesn't make it that fun. Most bicycles use the bottom deck to get between downtown and Waterfront Park to the Eastbank Esplanade.

TECHNICAL INFO: Through-truss double-lift bridge. Main span is 211 ft. (64 m) long, lower deck is 26 ft. (8 m) above water, upper deck is 72 ft. (22 m) above water, and there's 163 ft. (50 m) of total vertical clearance when both decks are fully raised.

Burnside Bridge *Burnside Street* The Burnside is a bascule bridge (drawbridge) that opened in 1926. Architecturally speaking, the most significant thing about the bridge are the twin towers at each end of its movable section, done up in Italian Renaissance style. Culturally speaking, the significant things about the bridge is what goes on UNDERNEATH it. Under its westside is the Saturday Market, Portland's famed tourist trap. Under its eastside is the world-renowned Burnside Skatepark.

USAGE: Automotive traffic, pedestrians, and bicycles.

OWNER: Multnomah County.

BICYCLE INFO: Bike lanes run in both directions on the bridge itself (the westside connection is a bit spotty, forcing you to merge suddenly with fast-moving traffic). Eastside access are parallel one-way streets (Burnside & Couch) with bike lanes.

TECHNICAL INFO: Total length is 2,308 ft. (703 m), center span is 252 ft. (77 m), and lowered bridge is 64 ft. (20 m) above water.

(cl)

Burnside Bridge

Morrison Bridge *Between SW Washington/Alder on the west, SE Morrison/ Belmont on the east* Opened in 1958, and replacing two previous bridges bearing the same name, the Morrison Bridge is a busy workhorse spanning downtown with the Central Eastside. It's yet another Portland drawbridge, a "Chicago Style" bascule bridge (see drawing for how it opens). Built during the "we need to build a lot of stuff fast" period of bridge engineering, the Morrison is not much to look at. The "air traffic control tower" styled bridge towers (with slanted windows) are this bridge's most distinctive features. The bridge is one of the largest mechanical structures in Oregon, due to its 940 ton (!) counterweights with 36 ft. tall gears located inside each of its piers.

USAGE: Automotive traffic, pedestrians, and bicycles.

OWNER: Multnomah County.

BICYCLE INFO: There's a bike path on the south side of the bridge with somewhat sketchy connections to SE Water and Yamhill, and SW Naito and Morrison.

TECHNICAL INFO: Total length is 760 ft. (232 m), and draw span is 284 ft. (87 m).

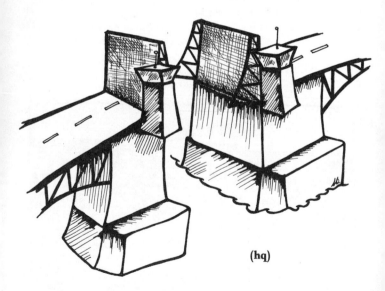

(hq)

Hawthorne Bridge *Connects SW Main/Madison on the west, SE Madison/Hawthorne on the east* Aah, the Hawthorne! This bridge is possibly Portlanders' most-favorite bridge, and it's at least the city's most distinctive bridge. Many postcards feature the photogenic structure, and it can even draw big-time Hollywood directors to shoot crappy big-budget movies here (see *The Hunted*). Anyways... The Hawthorne Bridge is a truss bridge with a vertical-lift span, and is the oldest vertical-lift bridge in operation in the U.S.! Built in 1910, it's the city's oldest highway bridge (and it still does a lot of work). A major rehabilitation effort was undertaken in 1998–1999, giving us the 10-foot wide sidewalks and green-and-red color scheme. The low clearance over the river means the drawbridge opens frequently, so it's common to be stuck waiting on the bridge.

USAGE: Automotive traffic, pedestrians, and bicycles.

OWNER: Multnomah County.

BICYCLE INFO: The Hawthorne is the city's busiest bicycle bridge with 1,500 bicycle crossings daily. The westside connects conveniently with Waterfront Park and the downtown grid, and the eastside connects to the Eastbank Esplanade and the Madison/Hawthorne bike lanes. Bicyclists must use the sidewalk (it's not fun riding on a steel grid deck)

TECHNICAL INFO: Total length is 1,382 ft. (421 m). Consists of five fixed spans and one vertical-lift span that's 244 ft. (74 m) long, and clearance is 49 ft. (15 m) above water.

(dw)

Marquam Bridge *Connects I-5 on both sides of the river* Opened in 1966, the Marquam Bridge introduced Portland to through traffic on I-5 between Vancouver, B.C. and Mexico. The double-deckered cantilever bridge sits high above the Willamette River, dominating the scenery around it. The bridge itself is boring—a victim of the "Vanilla School of Engineering" that built the nation's Interstate Highway System on the priciple that economy of design and cost trumps aesthetics. This issue infuriated many Portlanders at the time of its completion, and led to the Portland Art Commission's help with the design of the Fremont Bridge in 1973. Great views of the city and

Mt. Hood abound from this bridge if you're driving over it in a car. If you're a pedestrian or bicyclist, you're out of luck (at least until BridgePedal).

USAGE: Automotive traffic ONLY.

OWNER: State of Oregon.

BICYCLE INFO: Prohibited! The only legal time you can ride on it is during Bridge Pedal in the summer.

TECHNICAL INFO: Length of main span is 440 ft. (134 m), length of two side spans are 301 ft. (92 m) each, vertical clearance of the lower deck is 130 ft. (40 m) above the river, and the upper deck is 15 ft. (5 m) above the lower.

Tilikum Crossing, Bridge of the People *Connects MAX Light Rail between the Marquam and Ross Island Bridges* Portland's newest Willamette bridge, freshly opened in 2015! This bridge is unique for a couple of reasons: it's our only cable-stayed bridge, and it's the first major bridge in the U.S. built for transit, cycling, and pedestrians only. Yep, that's right, cars can't use this bridge! (TriMet buses can use it, along with an occasional emergency vehicle.) While the bike lanes on the bridge (and the connections when they hit land) are far from perfect, they're heaps better than ones on nearby Ross Island Bridge. "Tilikum" means "people" in the native local Chinook language.

USAGE: MAX Light rail, Portland Streetcar, TriMet buses, emergency vehicles, pedestrians, and bicycles. No private auto or truck use!

OWNER: TriMet.

BICYCLE INFO: Bike lanes adjoin the pedestrian walkway. Connects to SW Gibbs and Eastbank Esplanade.

TECHNICAL INFO: Cable-stayed bridge with a total length of 1,720 ft. (520 m). Main span is 780 ft. (240 m), total height (at towers) is 180 ft. (55 m), and vertical clearance above river is 77.5 ft. (23.6 m).

Ross Island Bridge *Connects ramp nonsense on the west side, Powell Blvd. (US 26) on the east* Opened in 1926, the Ross Island Bridge is named after the sandy isle in the Willamette directly to the south of it. Its cantilever-truss span is a subtle beauty (much like Portland itself): the more you look at it, the more you appreciate it. The Ross Island was the city's busiest bridge from its time of completion up until the opening of the Marquam Bridge.

USAGE: Automotive traffic, pedestrians, and bicycles.

OWNER: State of Oregon.

BICYCLE INFO: The Ross Island offers remedial bicycle facilities. Bicyclists must use a narrow sidewalk and then negotiate their way around a series of off-ramps on the westside (this can be pretty dangerous). ODOT rehabilitated the bridge a few years back, but improved the bicycle access very little, which seems to happen with all their recent bridge projects (see St. Johns). Since the opening of the Tilikum Crossing in 2015, there's not much reason to bike across this bridge any more.

TECHNICAL INFO: Longest span is 535 ft. (163m).

Sellwood Bridge *Connects SW Marquam/Riverside on the west, SE Tacoma on the east* The Sellwood Bridge, along with the St. Johns Bridge, are the least-seen Willamette-River bridges to the casual visitor, mostly due to their distance from center center. It's about five miles south of downtown, and is more useful for connecting to the far-reaches of the metro area than to the city itself. The original two-lane truss bridge opened in 1925. By the turn of the millennium, the bridge was overused beyond its capacity. Its capacity of 32 tons was lowered to 10 in 2004 after bridge inspectors found numerous cracks in its span. Not safe! So the county finally decided to build a new one, which they're currently constructing as I'm editing this guide! The new bridge will be a steel-deck arch bridge with much wider sidewalks than the old one, have the ability to carry a streetcar (if someone gets around to it), and have bike lanes to relieve cyclists! (Believe me, biking across the old bridge sucked.) The new bridge should be opened by spring of 2016, but we all know that schedules are meant to be broken.

USAGE: Automotive traffic, pedestrians, and bicycles.

OWNER: Multnomah County.

BICYCLE INFO: Bike lanes! (In 2016.)

TECHNICAL INFO ON THE OLD BRIDGE (New Bridge tech info not available at time of publication): Total length is 1,971 ft. (601 m) with four continuous spans, two center spans are 300 ft. (92 m) in length each, two outside spans measure 246 ft. (75 m), and clearance is 75 ft. (23 m) above river.

City Repair

Imagine this: You're cruising on your cruiser through the sunny Sunnyside neighborhood one sunshiney summer day. You're rolling eastward along SE Yamhill St., letting the gentle grip of gravity propel you down the shallow hill from SE 30th. As you approach the intersection of SE 33rd Ave., your eyes are caught by a bright mass of color plopped in the middle of the street. As you get closer, you notice the yellow is actually a giant sunflower painted onto the asphalt at the intersection! You stop in your tracks, puzzled. Then you notice that on each corner, there are large orange barrels with a wire sunflower growing out of it! And even curioser, on the NE corner, there's a small waterfall in someone's yard, and a community messageboard constructed of—straw bale? This is the part where you say to yourself: "What the hell's going on here?" City Repair is what's going on here.

What's City Repair, you may ask? According to its website: "The City Repair Project is a group of citizen activists creating public gathering places and helping others to creatively transform the places where they live." In plainer English, they are trying to bring back the public square, which has been long-dead (or was it stillborn?) in American urban planning. Since most of the U.S. (at least west of the Mississippi) is based on the grid system with its rigid traffic-only intersections, there's really no public place, save for parks, for people to meet and hang out. City Repair works with neighborhoods to repair intersections that will allow people to come together in a public space, meet their neighbors, communicate, share, and the like. The most visible manifestation of what they do is through two projects: Intersection Repair, and The Village Building Convergence. Traversing the town, you may see some of the cool things City Repair is responsible for, or has a hand in.

Memorial Lifehouse *SE corner of SE Taylor St. and SE 37th Ave.* On May 27, 1998, 27-year-old Matthew Schekel was riding his bicycle down Taylor when a delivery truck ran a stop sign on 37th, hitting and killing Matthew. After the accident, an impromptu memorial sprung up: two bicycle frames covered in flowers put into the dirt between sidewalk and street. In spring of 2002, City Repair built a more permanent installation. Getting the permission of the property owner at the corner, they built a "Memorial Lifehouse" directly into the retaining wall here. Made out of cob, the lifehouse has an "ecoroof," covered with plants that can absorb rainwater. At the base of the lifehouse is an alcove for random trinkets and other ephemera in tribute of Matthew. To the right is a bench covered in intricate glass mosaic and stonework. At the right end is a solar panel/bicycle wheel atop another tower. Planted into the lawn is a wheel with an account of Matthew's life and the project that brought this wonderful structure into being. I always pause

Memorial Lifehouse (sg)

when I ride by here, and reflect on the beauty of the memorial, and on how one stupid mistake can end someone's life.

Share-It Square *Intersection of SE Sherrett St. and SE 9th Ave.* This intersection repair was the first project City Repair worked on, way back in the dark ages of 1996. On the NE corner you'll find a community bulletin board, picnic table, a li'l stove shaped like a beehive, and a trade station where people can drop off or pick up produce, household items, etc. On the SW Corner, there's a "24-hour Tea Station" which provides free tea supposedly 24/7 via an airpot, plus a beautiful cob bench. On the NW corner, there's a small open "house" with toys for kids, and various books and magazines to peruse while you're hanging out here. And painted in the intersection itself is a big bullseye-esque pattern.

Sunnyside Piazza *Intersection of SE Yamhill St. and SE 33rd Ave.* This intersection saw its repairing begin in late 2001 with the painting of the sunflower. Since then, the piazza's most noticeable building was erected on its NE corner, with the message kiosk (that has a solar-powered light!) and a solar-powered fountain. There are also some yellow rainbarrels on the corner of this intersection. Check out the cool Victorian houses here as well.

Coffee, Tea, and the Like
North

Albina Press 4637 N Albina Ave. 503-555-1234 One of Portland's primo coffee joints. It's the type o' joint where the baristas consistently compete and win in those barista challenges. But don't be intimidated! It's a great place to check out, and to sip a coffee on a winter's day.

Arbor Lodge 1507 N Rosa Parks Way 503-289-1069 TheArborLodge.com Warm and light neighborhood spot with great coffee. Look for its custom cargo bike out front. (It's a Bullitt, if you are wondering.)

Blend Coffee Lounge 2710 N Killingsworth St. 503-473-8616 BlendCoffeepdx.com This cafe started originally on E Burnside, a spot that had seen many coffee shops over the years (Burnside Bean, Beehive, and Green Beans Cafe,whatever the hell it is now). Its North location opened about 10 years ago—the Burnside location finally sold, so this is the one and only Blend. Did anything I just say really matter to you, dear reader? Nope. But believe you me, the baristas at Blend know what they're doing, specializing in smooth espresso drinks. The space is a great place to hang, but if it's a nice day, get that coffee to go and head a few blocks west to the Willamette Bluffs!

Cup Coffee Co. 7540 N Interstate Ave. 503-477-9887 CupCoffeeCo.com Located in an old house just across from the Freddies. There are many nooks and crannies in there, so go hide yourself on a winter's day!

Cathedral Coffee 7530 N Willamette Blvd. 503-935-4312 CathedralCoffee. com Unfortunately, the farther out you get towards St. Johns, the slimmer the pickings for decent coffee. Cathedral opened a few years back to fill that void. The interior space manages a fine balance between inviting and industrial. You'll find lots of kids from nearby University of Portland studying here. And while any cafe near a college is guaranteed business, the coffee drinks here are actually great, so make a stop here on your bike ride to/from St. Johns!

Fresh Pot 4001 N Mississippi Ave. 503-284-8928 TheFreshPot.com The Fresh Pot has been the standby "good coffee" shop wherever it has been since it opened in the late '90s. While other coffee places may now be "sexier," you're not a true Portlander if you haven't spent time in one of its three locations. Yeah, it can be a bit of a scene, but the baristas are always great and friendly to a fault. And they know their coffee, so you can't go wrong. But the added bonus for you out-of-towners is you might just run into your favorite Portland "rock stars" here. Fun fact: The North location was used as the cafe setting in the 2007 film "Feast of Love" starring Morgan Freeman. (And no, I haven't seen the movie, so I can't tell you if it's good or not.)

Mr. Green Beans *3908 N Mississippi Ave. 503-288-8698 MrGreenBeanspdx. com* Not a cafe, but a coffee retailer selling roasted and unroasted beans, hence their name. It also has a metric ton of coffee making devices and coffee accessories. Do you need a replacement rubber gasket for your Bialetti moka pot? It's got it!

Posies Bakery and Cafe *8208 N Denver Ave. 503-289-1319 PosiesCafe. com* Kid-friendly cafe in the heart of Kenton. Go get some library books from the nearby branch, then spend a rainy day reading and drinking coffee!

Ristretto Roasters *3808 N Williams Ave. 503-288-8667 RistrettoRoasters. com* One of Portland's top coffee roasters. I miss the days of its cramped Beaumont location, and ad artwork done by Aaron Nelson Stenke, but things change, alas. What hasn't changed is its commitment to quality beans and coffee beverages.

Northeast

Case Study Coffee Roasters *5347 NE Sandy Blvd. 503-477-8221; 1422 NE Alberta St. 503-477-8221 CaseStudyCoffee.com* Nice cafe with good drinks and a big community table. Good place to meet up with friends, or grab some comics from nearby Cosmic Monkey and read 'em here!

Caffe Vita *2909 NE Alberta St. 503-954-2171 CaffeVita.com* Portland's outpost of the classic Seattle coffee-roaster chain. Not to be confused with Vita Cafe, the mostly veggie/vegan cafe located just two blocks down the street!

Extracto Coffee Roasters *2921 NE Killingsworth St. 503-281-1764; 1465 NE Prescott St. 503-284-1380 ExtractoCoffee.com* Coffee roastery and cafe specializing in espresso art. I also dig the empty "phone booth" at the Killingsworth location meant to be used by folks on their cell phones.

Goldrush Coffee Bar *2601 NE Martin Luther King Jr. Blvd. 503-460-6657* This coffee joint makes some smooth coffee, and some nice sandwiches as well. Internet access available, and plenty of cool pictures of the neighborhood "back in the day" that line the walls.

Heart Coffee Roasters *2211 E Burnside St. 503-206-6602 HeartRoasters. com* You can count on two things at this li'l joint: good coffee (they roast it themselves!), and it's going to be busy. So you know Heart knows its stuff!

Jim and Patty's *4951 NE Fremont St. 503-284-2121 JimandPattys.com* Do you remember Coffee People? Before Stumptown, Coffee People was Portland's coffee shop, with many locations around town. (Their tag line: Good coffee, no backtalk.) If you want to pretend that you were around "back in the day," find one of the Coffee People travel mugs (you could probably find one at Goodwill) and cart it around with you. Anyways, Jim and Patty Roberts were the "coffee people" of Coffee People. They sold the company in 1998, and Coffee People basically ceased to exist a few years later (thank you, Starbucks). Fun fact: The lone Coffee People still exists at the airport. After getting out of the coffee biz, Jim and Patty decided to come back! Now, besides good coffee (and presumably still no backtalk), they also serve some good breakfast. (Try that in most of Portland's coffee places!) And their specialty is Sour Cream Coffeecake.

Ristretto Roasters *555 NE Couch St. 503-284-6767 RistrettoRoasters. com* Besides coffee, the Couch location also features one beer on tap, plus bottled and canned beers to drink!

Seven Virtues *5936 NE Glisan St. 503-236-7763; 2705 NE Sandy Blvd SevenVirtuespdx.com* Great cafe serving good drinks and breakfast foods too. Fun fact: Seven Virtues used to get bagels Next Day Air'd from The Bronx years ago, when good bagel choices were slim. If that doesn't show a commitment to quality, I don't know what else will!

Tiny's Coffee (MLK) *2031 NE Martin Luther King Jr. Blvd. 503-467-4199 Tinys.Coffee* Bustling outpost of the popular coffee shop.

Townshend's Tea House *2223 NE Alberta St. 503-445-6699 TownshendsTea.com* Hundreds of tea options from herbal to white to black to green, all available hot or iced with cozy seating. Dry tea is also available for purchase by the pound. Kombucha, snacks, and bubble tea also available.

Woodlawn Coffee and Pastry *808 NE Dekum St. 503-954-2412 WoodlawnCoffee.com* Cafe and bakery right in the heart of the Woodlawn Triangle. It also has simple breakfast offerings, and a secret and changing "breakfast plate" that's not on the menu. So ask for it!

Southeast

Albina Press *5012 SE Hawthorne Blvd. 503-974-6584* See previous listing.

Bipartisan Café *7901 SE Stark St. 503-253-1051 BipartisanCafe.com* Yes, a good Portland coffee place only (gasp!) three blocks from 82nd Avenue. Bipartisan meets all the qualifications: Stumptown Coffee, good homemade pies, hardwood floors, big windows, an airy interior, and great staff. The presidential decorations (depicting most every president since there were presidents) may irk "staunch radical anarchists" (who pro'lly won't leave inner N/NE anyway) and there are quite a few "Christian Study Groups" meeting here at any given time, due to the proximity of several bible colleges in the area. But where else can you find an actual circa 2000 Palm Beach County

(Fla.) voting machine, with the infamous butterfly ballot? Well, where can you, wise guy?

Cellar Door Coffee Roasters *2001 SE 11th Ave. 503-234-7155 CellarDoorCoffee.com* You've seen its beans 'round town, now say hello to its awesome coffee-shop incarnation. Spectacular coffee and an assortment of in-house baked goods by a pastry chef extrordinaire.

Coava Coffee Roasters *1300 SE Grand Ave. 503-894-8134; 2631 SE Hawthorne Blvd. 503-894-8134 CoavaCoffee.com* One of Portland's best coffee roasters! And it's pronounced "co-vuh." Besides good coffee drinks, it also offers coffee supplies for sale. The Hawthorne location is a bit less austere and more cozy.

Five Points Coffee Roasters *3551 SE Division St. 503-453-0190 FivePointsCoffeeRoasters.com* Originally called Coffee Division (and in the location of the former Haven Coffee), Chris Larson opened this great coffee shop in 2011. It was one of the first shops to specialize in Chemex-brewed coffee. Now, it roasts some great coffee! Its Division location is spacious yet cozy, a good place to hang out for a bit and listen to some good music. And Five Points just opened a second location in John's Landing, which has increased the amount of good coffee in SW Portland by at least 25%! Fun Fact: I used to live with Chris.

The Fresh Pot *3729 SE Hawthorne Blvd. 503-232-8928 TheFreshPot.com* This cafe is inside Powell's on Hawthorne, so access the cafe via the main Powell's entrance (except when Powell's is closed, when you'll need to use the side entrance).

Palio Dessert House *1996 SE Ladd Ave. (at Ladd Circle) 503-232-9412 Palio-In-Ladds.com* This place rocks for location! It's smack dab in the middle of Ladd's Addition! While its coffee is not that exciting, the selling point is its dessert items. You won't get such a great cake selection at other cafes! Palio is open fairly late, especially when compared with most other Portland cafes that close by 6 PM. So you'll find the place hopping with late-night study sessions.

Pied Cow Coffeehouse *3244 SE Belmont St. 503-230-4866* If you're not satisfied with a typical coffee house and want more of an "experience," then come here. Located in a beautifully restored Victorian house, the Pied Cow serves some of the best hot drinks around. Espresso-based beverages are delicious and inexpensive (but HOT! Be careful of their glasses). Wine and beer are also available. Plus they have the "$50 Sundae," which is indeed fifty bucks. And it's humongous, so split it twelve ways! The décor inside is quite funky, and in the summertime you can sit outside in the garden. Good place to bring your out-of-town guests or someone you want to impress.

the pied cow

(cl)

Southeast Grind *1223 SE Powell Blvd 503-473-8703 SoutheastGrind.com*
As far as I know, this is Portland's only 24-hour coffee shop. You'll catch a
lot of Reedies studying here into the early morning. (Sorry East Coasters, we
don't have any Dunkin' Donuts.)

Stumptown Coffee Roasters *4525 SE Division St. 503-230-7702;
3356 SE Belmont St. 503-232-8889 StumptownCoffee.com* Okay, let's get
this over with: What was once the gold standard for Portland coffee, the
place that firmly put Portland on the World Coffee Map, is now owned by a
multinational conglomerate. (Yes, it was "bought by Peet's", but Peet's is owned
by a Luxembourg company that also owns Caribou Coffee...and Jimmy
Choo?) I had an internal debate as to whether or not to include Stumptown
because of this, but for many, they still personify not just Portland coffee,
but coffee in the 21st century. And yes, its coffee is still good (for now) and
available in many cafes. Sadly, Stumptown is no longer the small local roaster
that would never sell beans outside the city limits.

Sweetpea Bakery *1205 SE Stark St. 503-477-5916 SweetpeaBaking.com*
Anchor of the Vegan Mini Mall, Sweetpea serves up first-rate vegan baked
goods, drinks, soups, and a superb sandwich menu. Great place to relax and
ogle your favorite vegan-friendly folk.

TaborSpace *5441 SE Belmont St. 503-238-3904 TaborSpace.org* A nonprofit coffee shop located in Mt. Tabor Presbyterian Church. It's also host to events, so check its website for info.

Tao of Tea *3430 SE Belmont St. 503-736-0119 TaoofTea.com* Huge selection of tea, Asian-style snacks, and a calm atmosphere. It's also a tea wholesaler, so order online.

Townsend's Tea House *3531 SE Division St. 503-236-7772* See previous listing.

Tiny's Coffee *1412 SE 12th 503-239-5859 Tinys.Coffee* Stumptown coffee, good food (including some strange menu items), videogames, pinball, lively staff, and wifi. Inviting neighborhood feel, often with good music playing, monthly art openings, and a nice back patio.

The Ugly Mug *8017 SE 13th Ave 503-230-2010 uglymugpdx.com* It's always good to make a field trip to Sellwood every once in a while: the cruise alongside the Willamette is beautiful, the views of the city from Sellwood Blvd., the...coffee? Well, for the longest time, nothing really impressed me down in Sellwood, be it quality of coffee or atmosphere of shop. Luckily, the Ugly Mug came along. This joint has got the Stumptown, it's got the atmosphere, it's got the mug-shaped bike rack in front, and now it's got the beer and wine. I can get so amped up here it can almost make a trip to the Bins bearable. Almost!

Water Ave Coffee *1028 SE Water Ave. #145 (entrance on SE Taylor) 503-808-7083 WaterAvenueCoffee.com* One of Portland's premier coffee roasters. Grab a cup to go, and head on over to the river!

Southwest

An interesting thing to note: Many of the recommended coffee places in SW are second or third or fourth (etc.) locations of local coffee chains. You may think that these coffee places originated downtown and then expanded elsewhere across the city. But it's actually the reverse, as most of them started on the Eastside and then "branched" into downtown!

Case Study *802 SW 10th Ave. 503-477-8221* See previous listing.

Courier Coffee *923 SW Oak St. 503-545-6444 CourierCoffeeRoasters.com* A great early morning, gourmet coffee stop from a local bicycle-delivered roastery that is all the rage. Owned and operated by cool people.

Fehrenbacher Hof Coffee House *1225 SW 19th Ave. 503-223-4493* This is one of my favorite "hidden" coffeehouses in town. Tucked away in a corner not normally travelled to by the "hip" crowd (that'd be Goose Hollow), the Fehrenbacher serves up some great caffeinated beverages, and it always seems to have delicious baked goods at prices that can't be beat. For the budget conscious, it offers a "toast bar." Buy a couple slices o' bread, throw 'em in the toaster, and then slather with butter, jam, and/or peanut butter! (Yes, you can make a toasted PB&J sandwich!) The back room is a cozy place to while away a drizzly Northwestern afternoon, contentedly reading or drawing without worrying about running into someone you know (which can happen regularly at other places). And the Fehrenbacher is owned by the family of everyone's favorite eccentric ex-mayor Bud Clark. Whoop Whoop! (They also own the Goose Hollow Inn next door.)

Five Points Coffee Roasters *0614 SW Dakota St.* See previous listing. Note: That the zero in the address is important!

Fresh Pot *724 SW Washington St.* See previous listing.

Heart Coffee *537 SW 12th Ave. 503-224-0036* See previous listing.

Stumptown Coffee Roasters *128 SW 3rd Ave. at Ash 503-295-6144 StumptownCoffee.com* Downtown location serves coffee, wine, and beer. Longtime favorite hangout of bike messengers and those who like to look like (or at) bike messengers.

Northwest

Coffeehouse Northwest *1951 W Burnside St. 503-248-2133 SterlingCoffeeRoasters.com* Original outpost of Sterling Coffee Roasters, another good small roaster. This café is tiny but warm.

Coffee Time *712 NW 21st Ave. 503-497-1090 CoffeeTimePortland.com* Northwest Portland's infamous old-school, late-night coffeehouse. Rare is the moment you'll find this place empty of people, as this place is an epicenter of "cool" kids, armchair philosophers, artists, chess players, the suburban set, and everyone in between. Coffee prices are a bit steep. Coffee Time is like the "Rush" of Portland coffee shops: either people really like Coffee Time or they really don't, so be forewarned!

Jim and Patty's Coffee *Immediate Care Center: 2246 NW Lovejoy Ave. 503-477-8363* See previous listing.

Sterling Coffee Roasters *417 NW 21st Avenue 503-248-2133 SterlingCoffeeRoasters.com* See Coffeehouse Northwest listing for more info.

TeaZone *510 NW 11th Ave. 503-221-2130 TeaZone.com* European-style tea salon with a good selection of teas, plus those neat "bubble tea" drinks with tapioca pearls in them.

Ristretto Roasters *2181 NW Nicolai St. 503-227-2866 RistrettoRoasters. com* A bit out there in NW Industrial, but worth checking out for the cool setting. It's connected to Schoolhouse Electric. Lots of old industrial things to look at!

Grocery Stores, Supermarkets, and Food Co-ops

Fred Meyer (Note: There are too many of them to list here, so the following locations are ones in the central city.) Interstate: 7404 N Interstate Ave. 503-286-6751; Hollywood: 3030 NE Weidler St. (south of Broadway) 503-280-1300; Glisan: 6615 NE Glisan St. 503-797-6940; Hawthorne: 3805 SE Hawthorne Blvd. 503-872-3300 (I like to refer to this location as "The rock and roll Freddies."); Stadium: 100 NW 20th Pl. (at Burnside) 503-273-2004 (This location is referred to by Jello Biafra in the Dead Kennedys song "Night of the Living Rednecks.") FredMeyer.com This super-duper-market chain started out here way back in the day, but eventually got bought out by Ohio-based Kroger. You can buy all your ordinary, and not so ordinary (stores have an extensive line of natural foods as well), groceries here, as well as TVs, garden supplies, underwear, and bicycles. It's your all-purpose stop. If you ever need to buy clothes, paint, groceries, duct tape with animals on it, and trashy romance novels from the same store, this is the place for you. And locals refer to it as "Freddies."

New Seasons Market Arbor Lodge: 6400 N Interstate Ave. 503-467-4777; Williams: 3445 N Williams Ave. 503-528-2888; Concordia: 5320 NE 33rd Ave. 503-288-3838; Grant Park: 3210 NE Broadway 503-282-2080; Hawthorne: 4034 SE Hawthorne Blvd. 503-236-4800; Seven Corners 1954 SE Division St. 503-445-2888; Sellwood: 1214 SE Tacoma St. 503-230-4949; Woodstock: 4500 SE Woodstock Blvd. 503-771-9663; Slabtown: 2170 NW Raleigh St. 503-224-SLAB (7522) NewSeasonsMarket.com These upscale groceries were started in 1999 by the former owners of Nature's Northwest. These stores are a weird hybrid offering the healthy, fancy foods of Whole Foods and the co-ops, while also offering the more standard grocery-store fare of Safeway and Freddies. Nobody's exactly sure who "owns" New Seasons anymore, and they're aggressively expanding in Portland and beyond. Still, New Seasons has the best samples on the weekends, offering up tons of fruits, cheeses, breads, cooked foods, and sometimes beer and wine!

Cherry Sprout Produce 722 N Sumner St. (at Albina) 503-445-4959 CherrySprout.com Neighborhood produce store and more. Carries a wide range of organic and local produce as well as a smidgen of bulk items, medicinals and general foods. Excellent prices on produce and friendly atmosphere.

Green Zebra Grocery *3011 N Lombard St. 503-286-9325 GreenZebraGrocery.com* Only in Portland! Green Zebra is what would happen if you took a New Seasons or Whole Foods and put in the space the size of a large convenience store. So you know it's going to be a quick in-and-out, but with a better selection of food! It offers a salad bar, hot food bar, and deli counter, plus a growler fill station. Fun fact: Green Zebra only carries Oregon beers! And please don't confuse Green Zebra with the 1980's rock band Zebra, a third-tier Rush. (They never did tell me who's behind the door!) There's currently only one location in Kenton, but soon there'll be outposts in the Lloyd District and near PSU. And maybe someday on Division St.!

Trader Joe's *Hollywood: 4121 NE Halsey St. 503-284-4232; Southeast: 4715 SE 39th Ave. 503-777-1601; Northwest: 2122 NW Glisan St. 971-544-0788 TraderJoes.com* National chain of unique and inexpensive gourmet groceries. Not the best place for all-around shopping (its produce section is sparse, and stores lack the bulk-foods section that Wild Oats, New Seasons and the co-ops feature), but it's great for finding deals on stuff (including the ubiquitous "Three-Buck Chuck"). Good beer selection. If you're so inclined, it carries some of the best ever frozen microwaveable foods.

Alberta Co-op Grocery *1500 NE Alberta St. 503-287-4333 AlbertaGrocery. coop* This small grocery store began as a neighborhood natural-food ordering club. Good selection of local organic produce and baked goods, as well as the typical health-food-store selection of bulk items, medicinals, and general foods. Decent prices, especially on vegetables. Support local co-ops!

Food Fight! Vegan Grocery Store *1217 SE Stark St. 503-233-3910* Food Fight is a vegan junk-food store. The owners are nice and helpful, and there are many yummy things you can buy that are familiar, and others that you may have never seen before. But the number one reason Food Fight is amazing and brilliant is: it sells mysterious, Asian vegan meats! They're so good! Things like mushroom cake, golden roast, and ham are there, as well as other strange things that are labeled in non-English languages.

People's Food Co-op *3029 SE 21st Ave. 503-674-2642 Peoples.coop* Their slogan, "Food for People, Not Profit," says it all. Free of all meat products (including rennet). People's is the best place to buy food in the Southeast if you're hesitant (or unwilling) to support large chain stores. It carries a beautiful selection of local organic produce and a well-stocked bulk section. The prices tend to be a few cents more than those at the bigger shops in town, but the community atmosphere and environmentally conscious attitude of People's make shopping here worth it.

Sheridan Fruit Company *409 SE Martin Luther King Jr. Blvd. 503-236-2114 SheridanFruit.com* Local produce distributor that acts also as a neighborhood grocer. Pick up low-priced fruits and veggies here (organics and locally-grown stuff, too!). Sheridan has a great bulk-foods and beer selection, as well gourmet foods and a meat counter!

Food Front Cooperative Grocery *Northwest: 2375 NW Thurman St 503-222-5658; Hillsdale: 6344 SW Capitol Hwy 503-546-6559 FoodFront. coop* Natural-food coop market that has been around since 1972. Good place to pick up your organic produce and bulk food items. Its deli makes a swell lunch too! I always stop for provisions at the NW location on my way into Forest Park.

World Foods *830 NW Everett St. 503-802-0755 WorldFoodsPortland.com* Don't let its "fancy" location (Pearl District) and looks deceive you: World Foods is one of the best places in town to get international foods, especially Middle-Eastern foods. Its deli has fresh hummus, which will beat that container of whatever you bought from Freddies by a mile and change! Good beer, cheese, and chocolate selection too.

La Bouffe International Gourmet *8015 SE Stark St. 503-256-9576* Humble, little, Middle-Eastern market located next door to Ya Hala.

Proper Eats Market and Cafe *8638 N Lombard St. 503-445-2007* While a great vegan cafe (see restaurants), Proper Eats also serves as a small natural foods market that carries organic produce, soaps, bulk goods, household items, frozen foods, and of course beer. It's your best bet for this type of stuff up in St. Johns.

P's & Q's Market *1301 NE Dekum St. 503-894-8979* Small, upscale market with an assortment of groceries, produce, and beer. It also has a

Alberta Cooperative Grocery

(nb)

(dm)

deli counter and offers full meals with beers on tap. While prices are more than what you would pay elsewhere, this market does have good deals on some things like locally roasted coffee. Make sure you get one of the salted chocolate-chip cookies!

Hiking in and around Portland

by Paul Nama

In addition to a very rich city life, Portland is situated amidst amazing geography. Within 100 miles of Rip City one can see the ocean, waterfalls, high desert, mountains, and an active volcano!

The West Hills of Portland offer miles of interesting hiking trails which are accessible at various points by bus or MAX. At over 30 miles in length, the Wildwood Trail weaves its way through the West Hills connecting Hoyt Arboretum and Washighton Park to Forest Park. The trail starts a few hundred yards up the hill from the Washington Park MAX stop (served by the Blue and Red Line trains). Following the Wildwood Trail, you pass a viewpoint where Mt. St. Helens is visible on a clear day. Between 1.75 and two miles down the Wildwood Trail is another trail that leads to the Japanese Garden. On the trail, look carefully from above and you can see parts of this

Garden. Below the Japanese Garden is the Rose Garden, which supports a world-famous collection of roses. Continuing downhill is Washington Park and a fine city view, before ending up back in town. On the north side of Washington Park, you can catch the #20 Burnside bus back to downtown, or cross the street into the swanky Northwest neighborhood for the #15 bus or Portland Streetcar.

Built in 1914 by Henry Pittock, founder of *The Oregonian* newspaper, the Pittock Mansion is near the four-mile mark of the Wildwood Trail. For the interior-design-oriented folks, there is a tour of the house. But the real attraction is the backyard, which boasts a great view of Portland. On a clear day Mt. Hood completes the horizon; through the trees, Mt. St. Helens and Mt. Rainier are also visible. This is a fine place to have lunch or to take a break. There is a restroom and a drinking fountain at Pittock Mansion, but you may need to pack in your own lunch.

Coming down the hill from Pittock Mansion (the trail continues in the back of the parking lot), the Wildwood Trail goes downhill for about two miles before connecting with the Lower MacLeay Trail. This section is steep as it traverses through the forested canyons of the west hills. (There are many trails not described here that end in West Hills neighborhoods.) After crossing Balch Creek, the Wildwood Trail intersects with the Lower MacLeay Trail, which leads down the creek to MacLeay Park. MacLeay Park starts at NW 29th and Thurman, which is accessible via the #15 bus.

Instead of going all the way on the Wildwood Trail, the shorter path to Pittock Mansion is to cross through Hoyt Arboretum, picking up the Wildwood Trail near the three-mile mark. The first and third mile of the Wildwood Trail go through the Hoyt Arboretum, which covers 175 acres and contains plant life from around the world. There are posted maps, as well as maps for sale in the visitor center. Trails are clearly marked and, depending on what you want to see or how far you want to walk, you can create any hike in the arboretum. Personally, I like the redwoods, although they are not as big as those found near the Northern California coast.

The hikes between MacLeay Park and the start of the Wildwood Trail can be more or less difficult depending on which direction you go. The Washington Park MAX stop is about 710 feet above sea level; Pittock Mansion is about 950 feet above sea level; points in town (MacLeay Park, Burnside & NW 23rd) are about 100 feet above sea level. Starting at MacLeay Park and going up to Pittock Mansion would be the most challenging way to experience this trail system, whereas hiking from the start of the Wildwood Trail back to town is all downhill and much less strenuous. None of these trails are flat, so expect gentle grades constantly. Also, explore the Leif Erikson Trail. This is a multi-use trail, and there are many interesting connections between Leif Erikson and the Wildwood Trail. For a super-fun adventure, take the #4 bus to St. Johns, then walk over the St. Johns Bridge to the Ridge Trail. Take the Ridge Trail to Leif Erikson Trail, and then walk that back to town (roughly 10 miles total).

If you have access to a car, the ocean (Cape Lookout) or Mt. St. Helens (check out Truman's Ridge) are less than two hours from Portland. One hour to the east is the Columbia River Gorge, which is home to amazing geologic formations, breathtaking waterfalls, and endless hiking opportunities. The easiest way to tour the Gorge is to take I-84 east to Exit 35, where you can pick up the Historic Columbia River Highway (HCRH) going back west. From the west on the scenic highway (HCRH) is Horsetail Falls, Multnomah Falls, Wahkeena Falls, Latourell falls, and Crown Point Vista House (among many other destinations) before ending near Troutdale, east of Portland. Maps and hiking advice are available seven days a week from the Friends of Multnomah Falls in the visitor center at Multnomah Falls.

The trailhead at Horsetail Falls leads back to Ponytail Falls, where the trail crosses behind the waterfall before continuing on to Oneonta Gorge; Triple Falls is about 1.4 miles farther. The elevation there is about 700 feet, making this five mile out-and-back a moderate hike with a lot of spectacular things to see. Keep an eye out for Bigfoot as you hike the Northwest; Bigfoot's main stomping ground, Skamania County, is only a few miles down the river on the Washington side of the Gorge.

Oneonta Gorge is also accessible via the scenic highway. Oneonta Falls can be seen by hiking one mile up the gorge. Since this hike requires wading through Oneonta Creek, it is only recommended on a hot summer day, where you will probably encounter swarms of humanity with the same idea.

The next good hiking opportunity starts at Multnomah Falls. Multnomah Falls is the tallest in the Gorge (second highest continuously flowing waterfall in the continental U.S. at 620 feet) and has the largest crowds; go early for easier parking. The first 1.25 miles of this trail (441 feet) sucks because it is paved and crowded and very steep with no real view, but the country above Multnomah Falls is beautiful and less crowded. The loop between Multnomah and Wahkeena Falls passes five big waterfalls, and some nice gorge views over 5.5 miles (highpoint is about 1600 feet above sea level). To add more to this loop, follow trail #420C up to Devil's Rest. Here the crowd thins out even more (the vast majority of the crowd does not go beyond the top of Multnomah Falls) and provides some nice views over the 3.2 mile out-and-back, which peaks near 2400 feet above sea level. The Multnomah Falls area can also be accessed directly by Exit 31 off I-84.

Continuing west on the scenic highway near Exit 28 is Angel's Rest Trailhead. This hike is about 2.5 miles each way to an elevation of approximately 1600 feet. Along the way is Coopey Falls, and at the top is an amazing gorge view and a nice place to have dinner. This trail is best on a calm, clear day, as the top is not protected and can be very windy.

At Exit 28 there is westbound freeway access, or continue west on the scenic highway to see Latourell Falls. This is not the tallest waterfall in the Gorge (249 feet), but it is perhaps the most spectacular waterfall on the scenic highway. The trailhead leads to the top of Latourell Falls, and about one mile behind it is another waterfall. The trail leads over a bridge back to the other side of Latourell Falls. From there the trail goes through the woods, downhill, back across the scenic highway, through a park, under an old concrete bridge, and ends at the bottom of Latourell Falls. This loop is less strenuous than most Gorge hikes, providing a favorable ratio of sights to exertion that is perfect for less ambitious hikers.

Two-and-a-half miles west of Latourell Falls is the Crown Point Vista House; there is no hiking here, but it is a great place to get out of the car and take in a nice view both east and west down the Columbia River. There is access to the freeway a few miles west in Corbett, or for a nice country drive, stay on the scenic highway all the way to its end near Troutdale. This tour could also be done in reverse by taking I-84 to Exit 22 and following the signs to the eastbound Historic Columbia River Highway.

A few other points worth mentioning in the Gorge include Eagle Creek, Wahclella Falls, Bonneville Dam and Fish Hatchery, and the Bridge of the Gods. Located off Exit 41 on I-84, the Eagle Creek Trail is perhaps the most popular and spectacular hike in the Gorge. Most of the hike is on or above the creek, passing steep rock walls and numerous waterfalls (Punchbowl Falls at 2.5 miles and Tunnel Falls at six miles are the biggest). Parking lots on the scenic highway are free, but parking at Eagle Creek (or its neighbor Wahclella) requires a Northwest Forest Pass (available at the Multnomah Falls gift shop or online: $5 per day or $30 per year).

The Bonneville Dam is off Exit 40. There is a visitor center at the Dam with an underground viewing area where you can watch salmon traverse the fish ladder during their spawning season. Near the dam is a shipping lock. No stop to this area is complete without going to the nearby fish hatchery to see the sturgeons. Sturgeons are prehistoric bottom feeders that get quite large, and the pool at the fish hatchery contains Herman the Sturgeon, who is 9' 7" long!

From the Bonneville Dam exit on the south side of I-84 is the Wahclella Falls Trailhead. This trail is about one-mile long with a loop at the end, and is geographically similar to Eagle Creek. The Wahclella Falls Trail is breathtaking and highly recommended for people with shorter hiking ranges. The Columbia Gorge is nice to tour by car, but its true flavor is revealed to those who get out of the car and walk a little. Wahclella is a short and relatively flat, perfect for those whose health limits their ability to hike longer distances.

The town of Cascade Locks is at Exit 44. This is significant because the Pacific Crest Trail crosses between Oregon and Washington on the Bridge of the Gods, so this could be used as a starting point for longer backpacking trips. There is a park in Cascade Locks (behind the ice cream place) where you can see the old lock. If you do not want to take I-84 back to Portland, cross the Bridge of the Gods and take Washington State Route 14 west to I-205 southbound to Portland. There are many hiking trails and excellent gorge views on the Washington side of the Gorge; check out Beacon Rock or Cape Horn.

Weather in Portland is generally rainy in the winter and sunny in the summer. Winter hiking can be wet, but waterfalls are generally bigger in the rainy season. The Pacific Northwest is home to many types of wildflowers, which can be seen in the spring on many hikes (especially at Dog Mountain on the Washington side of the Gorge). Summer and fall can be less green but more comfortable; many trails change in character with the seasons.

Hopefully visitors and residents alike will take time to explore the variety of natural features that exist near Portland.

Hostels

Hostelling International-Portland, Hawthorne District *3031 SE Hawthorne Blvd.* 503-236-3380 *PortlandHostel.org* Located in a house built in 1909, this hostel is close to all the wonders Hawthorne Blvd. has to offer. Friendly staff, clean decor, spacious kitchen and living rooms, yard, garden, deck, covered porch, and an ecoroof! Linens included, no lockout/curfew, bike storage, bike rental, ample free parking, and wifi, as well as free breakfast, coffee and tea! Please note there is a $3 nightly surcharge for those not members of Hostelling International. Open all year with 24-hour access. Reservations are advisable any time of the year!

Hostelling International-Portland, Northwest Neighborhood *425 NW 18th Ave.* 503-241-2783 *NWPortlandHostel.com* This hostel is housed in a two historic buildings. Free pastries and bread. Kitchen, lockers, laundry, and Internet are available. Helpful and friendly staff can provide great information on things to see and do. Please note there is a $3 nightly surcharge for those not members of Hostelling International. Open all year with 24-hour access. Reservations are advisable any time of the year!

The Multnomah County Library System

Multnomah County Library *Central Library: 801 SW 10th Ave. 503-988-5123; Hillsdale Branch: 1525 SW Sunset Blvd. 503-988-5388; Hollywood Branch: 4040 NE Tillamook St. 503-988-5391 (This one's got a map of Beverly Cleary/Ramona the Brave landmarks in it!); Holgate Branch: 7905 SE Holgate Blvd. 503-988-5389; Albina Branch: 3605 NE 15th Ave. 503-988-5362; Belmont Branch: 1038 SE 39th Ave. 503-988-5382; Gregory Heights Branch: 7921 NE Sandy Blvd. 503-988-5386; Kenton Branch: 8226 N Denver Ave. 503-988-5370; North Portland Branch: 512 N Killingsworth St. at Commercial Ave. 503-988-5394 (This branch may be haunted!); Northwest Branch: 2300 NW Thurman St. 503-988-5560; Sellwood-Moreland Branch: 7860 SE 13th Ave. 503-988-5398; St. Johns Branch: 7510 N Charleston Ave. 503-988-5397 MultCoLib.org* Portland has a great library system, administered countywide. The "granddaddy" of the libraries is Central Library downtown, located at 801 SW 10th Ave. First opened in September 1913, and extensively renovated in 1996-97, Central Library houses over 875 tons of books(!) and other library materials. This branch has three floors; checkout the Fiction section, and the Beverly Cleary (she's from here, y'know!) Children's Room on the ground floor; Periodicals, Science, Business, Rare Books, Microfilm, and Government Documents on the second; Art, Music, and Humanities on the third. And of course, in this day and age, the library has many computers, some with Internet access that you can use for one hour (and despite the vast number of computers, they're ALWAYS BUSY!)

Title Wave Used Bookstore *216 NE Knott Street 503-988-5021* The former home of the Albina Branch, this bookstore sells remaindered books (books no longer in circulation), magazines, and CDs from the library system. A great place for deals!

Other Mercantile Operations

North

She-Bop *909 N Beech St. 503-473-8018 SheBoptheShop.com* A woman-owned sex-toy boutique that focuses on body-safe products and features workshops and educational resources. A rad selection of interesting materials in a friendly, safe, inspiring, and comfortable environment. Lots of accessories, condoms, and reading material as well.

Blue Moon Camera & Machine *8417 N Lombard St. 503-978-0333 BlueMoonCamera.com* A treasure and museum of sorts. Not your ordinary camera shop. Don't expect one-hour service or support for your digital photography needs. Blue Moon specializes in durable machines and quality processing. Staff sell what they shoot and print as if for themselves. A great resource for out-of-production film formats. Even if you're not into photography, go behold the typewriters. An impressive collection of refurbished manual writing appliances awaits you. Be nice to the staff and they may let you pet the typewriters.

Northeast

Collage *1639 NE Alberta St. 503-249-2190 Collagepdx.blogspot.com* Locally owned, extensive arts-and-crafts store conveniently located on Alberta St. Friendly staff and competitive prices.

Southeast

I've Been Framed *4950 SE Foster Rd.503-775-2651 IveBeenFramedpdx.com* This gem of an art shop is found at the unlikely intersection of Foster and Powell. Possibly some of the cheapest finds in the area, with a really friendly staff. Unlike places like Utrecht (er...Blicks), I've Been Framed focuses less on a standardized selection and more on closeouts it gets for cheap. So you'll never know what you'll find here!

Muse Art and Design *4220 SE Hawthorne Blvd. 503-231-8704 MuseArtandDesign.com* Finally! An art-supply shop on Hawthorne! Muse is a nice li'l store that will keep most artists satisfied. It also offers a free library containing titles on art, artists, techniques, materials, and eclectic visual references. Plus, exhibit art by local artists.

Andy and Bax *324 SE Grand Ave. 503-234-7538* Portland's oldest army-navy store opened in 1947! It's got most everything you need for clothing yourself for an urban expedition. I end up here quite often. It's my favorite place for winter wear: all the hats, wooly socks, gloves, wool pants, and thermal underwear you can possibly need. Like most army-navy joints, there's a bounty of surplus clothing items for cheap. Who knows what values lie in them there bins? And if (insert political leader name here) comes to town, this is where you can pick up gas masks so you don't get tear-gassed!

Next Adventure 426 SE Grand Ave. 503-233-0706 NextAdventure.net Billing itself as "Portland's alternative outdoor store" (since the '90s...how alternative), Next Adventure is, for want for a better term, Portland's version of REI. You'll find lots of the same types of stuff that you would find at that chain, except Next Adventure often has better prices since much of their stock is from closeouts. So if you see something here today, grab it, because it may be gone tomorrow, and it may never be restocked! The best bet is to hit up its Bargain Basement where everything is used and are at dirt-cheap prices! And if you have outdoor gear that you want to get rid of, you can sell it to the Bargain Basement! (Note: You only get store credit if you do that.) Next Adventure also has a paddle-sports center a few blocks away on SE Sandy Blvd.

Avant Garden Vintage Thrift 2853 SE Stark St. 503-283-4184 More on the vintage side than the usual junk-shop thrift, prices here are equitable and there's a wide assortment of styles and eras to choose from regarding clothing and home decór. The well-traveled proprietor has a number of odds and ends from her trips abroad, including Asian movie posters. Just ask and she can provide you with summaries of the film plots! Strangest of all are the vintage Chairman Mao alarm clocks. Avant Garden provides free pickup for donations.

The Bins (a.k.a. Goodwill Outlet) 1740 SE Ochoco St. (near McLaughlin) 503-230-2076 You have to be in a special mood to go to the "bins." Are you ready to get your hands dirty enough that touching your face afterward could lead to certain death? Ready to punch your way out if you've got an exceptional find? Then you're prepared for this amazing thrifting adventure. At the bins you buy clothes by the pound, and housewares and books for even less. It takes a lot of digging (as there are actual 100 foot long bins of unsorted merchandise for you to look through), but at times, you could find amazing things for insanely cheap prices. Watch out for the daring old women who race to the newest merchandise and will gladly knock you on the ground and step on your face if it can get them closer to that vintage mohair sweater!

Northwest

Ground Kontrol 511 NW Couch St. 503-796-9364 GroundKontrol.com The only retrocade in the Northwest. It also buys and sells old video-game systems, and also serves beer! So if you're looking for an Atari 2600 with that pint of PBR, come here.

William Temple House Thrift Store *2230 NW Glisan St. 503-222-3328* This place is quite unsnooty and chock-full of useful and/or frivolous gear. The range of household décor is especially good, compared even to the Goodwill store at 2215 W Burnside. Be sure to look in the display areas at the checkout counter for even more wacky stuff. Clothing variety is reasonable but the racks are chaotic and crowded together. This store has occasional bag sales as well.

Southwest

SCRAP *1736 SW Alder St. 503-294-0769 Scrappdx.org* SCRAP is an acronym of the "School and Community Reuse Action Project." Staff and volunteers collect reusable items from businesses and donations, and distribute them to educators, artists, families, and kids for low-to-no cost. SCRAP is an awesome place to find neat supplies for all sorts of projects. The inventory is constantly changing. You might find fabric, paper, wire, tile, sticker vinyl, office supplies, or any other miscellaneous treasures. Store also hosts workshops and has an area set aside for workspace for people to create in-shop. Big bonus for the friendly knowledgeable staff! And there are volunteer opportunities if you are interested.

(bo)

Parks

North

Kelley Point Park *All the way at the north-western most point of N Marine Drive where it meets N Lombard* Sometimes, failure is good. Back in the 1840s, when there were several towns along the Willamette vying to be "the city" of the Northwest, New Englander Hall J. Kelley attempted to build "the Manhattan of the Northwest" at what is now this park, sight unseen. It looks so logical on a map; this is where the Willamette meets the Columbia. But the reality of trying to build a town on low, swampy land prone to flooding proved too much for even the hardiest of New Englanders, and Kelley gave up. The land laid fallow for over a century, owned but not really used by the Port of Portland, until the Parks Department bought the "Point" in 1984. This small patch of wooded sand dunes provides good boat watching opportunities—you can see many ocean-bound freighters pass by here. (And to think what might have been if Kelley had succeeded!) Use N Marine Drive to get here (there's a bike path paralleling the street).

Peninsula Park *Between N Ainsworth, N Kerby, N Rosa Parks, and N Albina* Known for its swimming pools, community center, gazebo-like octagonal bandstand, fountains, and the city's first rose garden, which features 75 varieties of roses. (The International Rose Test Garden in Washington Park is the more famous and most popular rose garden in town). Peninsula Park was originally owned by local businesswoman "Liverpool Liz," when it was a roadhouse and horse racetrack. In the 1950s, the city zoo housed its penguins in the center's pool for six months because the zoo lacked the proper facilities when the birds arrived from Antarctica. Because of this, some old-timers still call it Penguin Park! Johnny Cash once had a picnic here.

Greetings from
PENINSULA PARK
NORTH PORTLAND

Skidmore Bluffs (a.k.a. "Mocks Crest Property") *2206 N. Skidmore Terrace (west of Overlook Blvd.)* In the past, this obscure park was a guarded secret. Well, what's popularly known as the "Skidmore Bluffs" isn't so secret anymore. This is basically a patch of grass at the west end of Skidmore, sitting on Mocks Crest, the bluff overlooking the Willamette River below. You won't find softball fields or rose gardens here, just some good views in Portland. You'll have downtown and Forest Park on the opposite bank, and the industrial riverside areas and Union Pacific's Albina (Train) Yard directly below (which explains why this spot is popular with the hobos). It's a great spot to watch the sun set over the West Hills. But it can be quite the scene on summer nights (think several hundred people, plus their dogs), which has caused friction with the neighbors.

The Horseshoe N Willamette Blvd. between Ainsworth and Killingsworth This patch of greenspace is a bit more obscure than the Skidmore Bluffs, yet easier to get to. It's not an official park (it's owned by the Bureau of Environmental Services) so it doesn't even have a name. I call it "The Horseshoe" because it's inside a big horseshoe curve on N Willamette Blvd. The bottomland is fill created by a long-closed dump. This part of the "park" is popular with dogs (it's a de facto off-leash area.) Atop the bluff is a grassy spot with a lone, dead madrona tree. It's a popular spot for picnics and sunsets, yet nowhere near as popular as the Skidmore Bluffs. So don't ruin this one, Portland! And look for "the face" embedded in the side of the hill!

Cathedral Park N. Edison and Pittsburgh A park right directly underneath the eastside of the St. Johns Bridge. The name of the park and surrounding neighborhood is derived from the Gothic towers of the bridge, reminiscent of an old cathedral. It's a great place to catch views of the bridge, the West Hills, and the river's traffic. Don't forget about the dock going out into the river, and the stormwater gardens at the adjoining Portland Water Pollution Lab. A scene from My Own Private Idaho was filmed here. Access via N Baltimore Ave., west of downtown St. Johns.

Columbia Park N. Lombard and Woolsey Historically, this was the first park that was created by the short-lived City of Albina. Picnic areas, ball courts, and tons and tons of Douglas firs. Also includes a pool.

Smith and Bybee Lakes Park Lying on the floodplain of the Columbia, Smith and Bybee Lakes is a freshwater estuary at the convergence of the Columbia River and Columbia Slough. This marshy area is good for observing a variety of wildlife, or just for chilling out and getting away from the heaviness of urban living for a bit. If it weren't for the constant drone of I-5 traffic (a couple miles off, even) and the occasional train noise, you'd think you were far from the city. (In reality, it's only about eight miles from downtown.) A paved path leads from the entry point to a couple of enclosed bird-watching shelters. The entrance is off of N Marine Drive and west of N Portland Road (a couple miles east of Kelley Point Park).

Pier Park N Lombard St. and Bruce Ave. This large park tucked away on the far end of St. Johns is a hidden jewel. It contains a skate park, a disc-golf course, tall Douglas firs, meandering paths, and acres and acres of rolling hillocks. Oh, there's also a pool here. Despite the park's name, it's not on the river, and there's never been a pier here. (The park is named after former Parks Commissioner Sylvester Charles Pier.) The park is used in the filming of the TV series *Grimm* as the Black Forest. A brand-new footbridge crosses over the Union Pacific tracks to adjoining Chimney Park, the former city incinerator, and then the home of the City Archives. Neither of those places are here anymore, but the building still remains.

Overlook Park *N Interstate Ave. at Fremont St.* Basically a big field with amenities, this park is a good spot to get a view of the city below, hence its name. Check out the cool stone picnic structure when you're here.

Northeast

Alberta Park *NE 22nd and Killingsworth* Despite it's name, it is NOT located on Alberta St., so don't be fooled! Shady spaces and sports facilities can be found here.

Grant Park *NE 33rd Ave. and US Grant Pl.* The neighborhood of Grant Park was named after the park Grant Park, which was named after Grant School that was named after President Ulysses S. Grant. Pretty exciting, huh? Grant Park is your standard, early 20th-century-type park, so it's not remarkable in itself, except for one exceptional landmark—the Ramona the Brave Statue Garden. The protagonist for the popular series of children's books authored by Beverly Cleary, Ramona (and Cleary) adventured in this very neighborhood. Ramona's fictional residence was on NE Klickitat St., just a few blocks north of the park. In fact, some of Ramona's adventures involve this park! In 1995, Portland immortalized Ramona, her friend Henry, and her dog Ribsy by placing bronze statues of them here.

Irving Park *NE Fremont St. and NE 7th Ave.* Possibly inner Northeast's most popular park. Ball fields, picnic benches, gorgeous trees, basketball courts, and crazed dogs in the off-leash area populate this green spot.

Fernhill Park *NE 37th Ave. at NE Ainsworth St.* A big, expansive park with ball fields and playgrounds. Its biggest selling point, quite possibly, is the wooded hillocks to the north of the park. Dogs love it here!

Rose City Park and Golf Course *NE Tillamook St. and NE 72nd Dr.* I'm not one to extol golf courses, but the big feature here is the view. This is the only spot on the Alameda Ridge that is greenspace, so from atop the bluff along NE Sacramento St. you can get good views of Mt. Tabor and Mt. Hood (if it isn't cloudy, of course.) There's also a cool but rough trail that runs along the north side of the golf course, under the bluff.

Khunamokwst Park *NE Alberta St. and NE 52nd Ave.* Portland's newest park! Cully is possibly the most underserved neighborhood west of 82nd when it comes to parks (there were none before this one) so this needed greenspace is much appreciated. It'll take a couple years before that sparkling newness gets replaced with a more grown-in feel, but enjoy the skatepark, the barrier free play area, rain gardens, and the covered picnic areas. *Khunamokwst* is a Chinook wawa name meaning "together", and is pronounced KAHN-ah-mockst.

Rocky Butte *NE Rocky Butte Dr.* While not the highest spot on the east side of Portland (that honor goes to Mount Tabor), it does have the best view of any of the volcanic buttes that pepper the landscape. Atop the Butte is Joseph Wood Hill Park, a small spot surrounded by impressive stone walls, giving it a castle-like appearance. The park's stone walls and the road to the top were built during the Depression by the Works Progress Administration. Just think about this when you're looking at the impressive stone work: all of it was done by hand, and it's not even a century old! But even more impressive than the stone work is the view, as you get a near 360-degree panorama, with Mount St. Helens, Mount Hood, Mount Tabor, Portland International Airport, the entrance to the Columbia River Gorge, and downtown visible. It makes quite the scenic backdrop for pictures, so on a nice day you'll probably see a wedding party in full regalia here. Also, check out the cool airway beacon towering above it all. Not a radio tower, but a revolving light that was placed here in the early days of aviation, when pilots flew by sight alone. While it's not used for aviation purposes anymore, the light still comes on at night (a dimmer version than in the past), visible from a good part of NE. A few items of note: There are no bathrooms or water at the top, just a trash can. And while people refer to the top as Rocky Butte Park, it's listed on maps as Joseph Wood Hill Park. You may also see a listing for "Rocky Butte State Park" on some maps, but it's just the undeveloped east side of the hill closest to I-205 and owned by the state.

Southeast

Col. Summers Park *SE Belmont St. and SE 20th Ave.* The Buckman neighborhood's local park, named after a hero of some war. (And watch out! People commonly misspell it as Sumner, Sumpter, or Sanders.) There's hella sports facilities here, including a tennis court, a baseball field, and a basketball court. There's also a community garden. It's possibly the inner SE's most popular mass-gathering spot, and the home to Monday Funday and Food Not Bombs.

Creston Park *SE 44th Ave. and SE Powell Blvd.* Despite being on a major traffic artery (Powell Blvd.), Creston Park's tall Douglas firs and landscaping provide a shady respite from the urban world. Plenty of room for a picnic and there's an off-leash dog park. Also, there's an outdoor pool open in the summer.

Crystal Springs Rhododendron Garden *SE 28th Ave. one block north of Woodstock Blvd. 503-771-8386* Located on seven acres just west of Reed College, Crystal Springs Rhododendron Garden features more than 2,500 rhododendrons, azaleas, and companion plants. Spring-fed Crystal Springs Lake surrounds much of the garden, attracting many species of birds and waterfowl. The winding paths and wooded knolls provide good places to get away and have personal time, if you want. Admission is free to all from the day after Labor Day through the month of February. A $4 admission fee is charged between 10 AM–6 PM, Wednesday through Sunday, from March through Labor Day. Admission is free for children under 12.

Eastbank Esplanade A path lying along the east bank of the Willamette River between the Steel and Hawthorne bridges that opened in 2001. This area used to be full of warehouses, just like on the westside of the river, but were torn down in the 1960s to make way for a freeway (Interstate 5). Unfortunately, that freeway still remains. But the city did manage to build a pathway regardless. Now you can cruise both banks of the river! There are some cool historical markers along the path. And the 1,200-foot-long floating walkway (just north of the Burnside Bridge) is the longest floating walkway in the United States. Watch out, though, because it gets crowded on nice weekend days and around weekday lunch hours, and speed-demon cyclists barrel down the pathways during rush hours. Waterfront Park is connected to the Eastbank Esplande by the pathways along the Steel Bridge (lower deck)

Laurelhurst Park (sg)

and Hawthorne Bridge. Keep on heading south past the Tilikum Bridge to connect to the Springwater Corridor.

Kenilworth Park *SE 34th Ave. and SE Holgate Blvd.* Kenilworth Park was built in the teens, and it reflects the "City Beautiful" design sense of the time. Its curvy paths, tall trees, and grassy ravines at the north end make it like a Laurelhurst Park in minature. There's also a great overlook on its west side where you can catch the sun setting.

Laurelhurst Park *SE Stark St. and SE Cesar Chavez Blvd. (39th)* Besides Mount Tabor, Laurelhurst Park is considered Southeast's signature park, and a great example of the City Beautiful era of park development. Built in the 1910s on property originally owned by mayor William S. Ladd, this park is often mistaken for one designed by the Olmsteds, the prominent park architects of the modern era. It was developed by Emanuel Mische, Portland's Park Superintendent from 1908–1914, who happened to work for, and learn from, the Olmsteds before landing the job. So, this park (and others he designed) is definitely Olmsted-inspired. The centerpiece of the park is Firwood Lake, one of the few bodies of water that remains in SE, and a popular spot for ducks. (The city discourages the feeding of said ducks because the pond can only support so many of them.) Come to Laurelhurst and meander its paths through groves of trees and rhododendrons. And when that rare snow hits, come watch kids sled down the slopes on the west side.

Lone Fir Cemetery *SE Stark St. and SE 26th Ave. Access points: from SE Salmon east of SE 60th, from the east at SE Harrison west of SE 70th, from the north at SE 69th and Yamhill (the 15 bus stops here.)* Lone Fir is administered by Metro, the regional government of the Portland metropolitan area. It's technically not a park, but it's a great place to wander around and bring out your goth side. Lone Fir is Portland's oldest continuously-used cemetery, and is now a de facto arboretum, with 500 trees representing 67 species. About 25,000 bodies are buried here. During Halloween, there's a very popular tour, so get your tickets early!

Mount Tabor *SE 69th Ave. and Yamhill St.* This 643-foot high hill was formed by volcanic activity. In fact, it's an extinct volcano—one of the few extinct volcanoes to be found within an American city. This mount could have been eaten up by the expanding development of the city of Portland, but famed park designers the Olmsted Brothers recognized the significance of this place, and urged the city to protect Mount Tabor by turning it into a city park. We can thank the Olmsteds today for their foresight, because Tabor offers one of the best views of the city. And its forested slopes are a great place to unwind. The windy road on the westside is closed to traffic, so it's a great place to "bomb" (to appropriate the Zoobomber's lingo for biking down steep grades). All auto traffic is barred from the park on Wednesday and every day after 10 PM! The beautiful open reservoirs are no longer used for drinking water (thanks, 9/11), and were decommisioned at the end of 2015. Plans to restore and preserve the resevoir are underway.

The Springwater Corridor Trail This linear park starts at the end of the Eastbank Esplanade just south of 'the Tilikum Bridge, heads south along the Willamette River, paralleling railroad tracks down to the Sellwood neighborhood, and then heads east through Gresham and all the way to the exotic "town" of Boring (yes, that IS its real name) in northern Clackamas County. This route was originally an interurban trolley line (alternately known as the the "Springwater" Line or the "Bellrose" Line) built in 1903 and discontinued in 1958. In the 1990s, the city of Portland and Metro (the city's regional government) acquired the unused rail line and converted it into a park. Now, instead of steel rails and ties, we have a paved 10-foot-wide path that you can walk, bike, skateboard, etc. The length of the path is approximately 21-miles long, and is now paved the whole way.

Beggars-Tick Wildlife Refuge *SE 111th at Springwater Corridor Trail* This small park features a wide variety of habitats including open water, shrub/scrub marsh, cattail/smartweed marsh, and forested wetland. The refuge also serves as a wintering spot for waterfowl.

Leach Botanical Gardens *6704 SE 122 Ave. 503-823-9503* Practically unknown by most of the folks I know, this plant park is hidden in a wooden hollow along Johnson Creek south of Foster Road. The nine-acre garden features a collection of over 2,000 species of plants, many of which are Northwest natives. Also featured is a composting-demonstration site. To get there from the Springwater Trail, go south along SE 122nd, crossing Powell. Be careful, it's a windy road!

Oaks Amusement Park *At the end of SE Oaks Park Way off SE Spokane St. (by the Sellwood Bridge) 503-233-5777; Rink: 503-236-5722* Once known as the "Coney Island of the Northwest," Oaks Park originally opened on May 30, 1905, making it one of the oldest amusement parks in the country, and the only amusement park in Portland. Designed as a trolley park (a recreational area along or at the end of trolley or streetcar lines that were popular in the early 1900s), most of its visitors "back in the day" disembarked from trolley cars which traveled from downtown Portland to Oregon City. Though the trolleys are long gone, their tracks are still here, and the park is sandwiched between them and the Willamette River. The amusement-park rides are still here, so if you're in the mood for good ol' carney-style fun in the summer, this is the place. The rides are in operation spring to early fall (daily in summer, weekends-only any other time). Don't forget the roller rink, which is open year-round! And there's a new miniature golf course!

Oaks Bottom Wildlife Refuge *SE 7th Ave and Sellwood Blvd.* This green area, wedged between the Willamette River and the Sellwood neighborhood, is an undeveloped park where you can see what the banks of the river looked like before the city was born. A mostly unpaved trail runs the eastern length of the park, starting at the SE Milwaukie Ave. and SE Mitchell entrance. Great place for birdwatching!

Reed College Canyon *Access from Botsford Drive off SE 28th (just north of Woodstock)* Despite what you may think of Reed College and its students (Reedies), the campus is a pretty nice place to go. Reed Canyon, a 26-acre natural area running lengthwise west/east through the heart of the campus, is its jewel. Crystal Springs Creek runs through the canyon—its source is a spring near SE 37th in the east—flowing westward to Johnson Creek. This stream is the last free-flowing one in this part of town, and its lake is "the only naturally occurring pond (or lake) remaining in the inner-city area." There's a nature trail that circles the ravine and is a great respite from the urban-ness that surrounds it. The lush canopy of trees above the steep sides of the ravine provide great relief on a hot summer day. If you don't want to enter from the main entrance, there are a couple of sneak entrances at the dead end of SE 37th Ave., a couple blocks south of Steele, and at the dead end of SE Reedway just to the west of 39th.

Sellwood Park *Enter at SE 7th Ave. two blocks north of Tacoma St.* Sellwood is your typical Portland park, complete with ball fields, picnic areas,

YOU JUST BE HIS TALL TO ENTER

Oaks Amusement Park (cm)

restrooms, and Douglas Firs. It adjoins Oaks Bottom Wildlife Refuge, Oaks Park, and Sellwood Riverfront Park.

Sellwood Riverfront Park *Enter at SE Spokane and SE 6th at foot of Sellwood Bridge* This park is on the banks of the Willamette River in far SE Portland. Good place to picnic and watch the boats on the river (there's a boat launch here as well.) A small sandy beach offers swimming access on a hot summer day.

Tideman Johnson Park *Along the Springwater Corridor Trail, west of SE 45th Ave.* Named after a pioneer family, this li'l park is nestled in a gorge along the Johnson Creek. Mostly in its natural state, this wooded secluded area is a nice hideaway when the city gets too much for ya, especially in the summer when you can stick your feet in the cool water. Also good for observing Johnson Creek, the only significant brook on the east side of town. Check out the cool stone wall and dam on the north side of the Springwater Corridor, built by the WPA (Works Progress Administration) during the Depression.

Powell Butte *SE Powell Blvd. and SE 162nd Ave.* This one is a bit distant for most folks, but totally worth it if you make the trek. Powell Butte is one of the many small hills formed by volcanic activity scattered about the east side like Mount Tabor and Rocky Butte. Powell Butte has been mostly left in a natural state. The glaring exception are the underground water tanks that provide Portland's drinking water. Its steep slopes are forested with great stands of Douglas fir and cedar, leading one SoCal visitor to exclaim that it was like the Ewok planet. Atop the butte is a large open meadow (with remnant orchard) that affords expansive views of everything, including the hard to spot (from Portland) Mount Jefferson! Many of the trails are open to bicycles, making it one of the few city parks you can legally mountain bike, though lots of mountain bikers diss these trails since they're not "technical" enough. And a few trails are open to horses. There's an alternate entrance from the south of the Springwater Corridor Trail.

Mount Scott Park *SE Harold St. and SE 72nd Ave.* This shady park with a canopy of Douglas firs is a perfect spot for a picnic on a hot summer day. The pool inside the community center is even more perfect for summer.

Ed Benedict Park *SE Powell Blvd. and SE 100th Ave.* This park is a bit out there, but easily accessible via transit. (SE Powell Blvd. station on MAX Green Line) The land that makes up the park was originially intended for the controversial and cancelled Mount Hood Freeway. Its biggest selling point is its skatepark, which features 18,000 sq. ft. of street skating with ledges, edges, stairs, rails, and banks. Also in the park is the Portland Memory Garden, an enclosed spot that's designed for those who have memory issues. The garden is level and quiet, and only has one entrance/exit.

Southwest

Council Crest Park SW Council Crest Dr. This hill is the highest point in the city at 1,073 feet (327 meters). Back in the day (1907–1929), there was an amusement park here—a trolley park similar to Oaks Park. You can see four snow-capped peaks (St. Helens, Rainier, Adams, and Hood) from this vantage point, as well as 3,000 square miles of land and rivers, plus the city itself. (Of course, that's if it's sunny out!). Council Crest is also along the Marquam Trail.

Gabriel Park SW 45th Ave. and SW Vermont St. This large park situated on the edge of Multnomah Village has plenty of park things like ball courts and off-leash dog areas. Running through the middle of the park is a creek with wooded natural areas surrounding it. (I wish some Eastside parks had this feature!) If you find yourself out this way, Gabriel Park is a to-do.

Hoyt Arboretum 4000 SW Fairview Blvd. 503-865-8733 A tree-hugger's paradise! This is a 214-acre "tree museum" on the western tip of Washington Park. with 4,300 different trees and over 800 types of shrubs on display. The Arboretum has the largest collection of coniferous (boreal) trees anywhere in the world. The collection includes rare trees, like the long-thought-to-be-extinct dawn redwood from China, plus traditional west-coast team-players giant sequoias, coast redwoods, and Douglas firs. Learn about our friends the trees whilst romping through a peaceful environment.

Ira Keller (Forecourt) Fountain SW Clay St. at SW 3rd Ave. During Portland's urban-renewal era in the mid 1950s to early 1970s, this parcel of land across from Civic Auditorium was acquired by the city for a park. Designed by Angela Danadjieva in 1968, and completed in 1970, the multi-tiered, modernist-designed fountain became an instant hit in town and abroad. (It also atracted "the hippies," which didn't please City Councillors like Frank Ivancie.) In 1978, Forecourt Fountain was renamed for Ira Keller, the first director of the Portland Development Commission (1958–1972) who, with then-mayor Terry Shrunk (1957-1973), was most responsible for urban renewal in Portland. Keller knew how to get his way, and projects like South Auditorium and Memorial Coliseum reflect that. Ponder that as you stare into the recirculating waters. Or take a dip on a hot day!

The Park Blocks North: along NW Park between W Burnside and NW Glisan; South: along SW Park between SW Salmon and Portland State University On the other side of the country, the Park Blocks would be referred to as "greens." These elm-lined parks are great places to take a leisurely stroll and to have a picnic lunch amongst the hustle and bustle of downtown. Say hello to the gold elephant on the north end!

Pioneer Square *Bounded by SW Morrison St., SW Broadway, SW Yamhill, and SW 6th Ave.* The city's boosters refer to this area as the "living room of Portland." Originally the site of the Portland Hotel, the grandest of all hotels in the city until it was torn down in 1951 to make way for a...parking lot, Pioneer Square was created in the 1980s as a space for public use downtown. It's the central meeting place of town, done in a European manner. This is probably the best place for people watching in town! The Portland Transit Mall and MAX lines intersect here.

Salmon St. Spring *SW Front and SW Salmon St.* Crazy kids (and the young at heart) ride their bikes through the center of this fountain on summer days. It's like running through sprinklers.

Terwilliger Parkway and Bike Lanes This linear park stretches for a couple miles along SW Terwilliger Blvd. from SW Barbur Blvd. and northward to almost I-405. In the early 20th century the city asked famed landscape architects the Olmsted Brothers to come to town and lay out a "grand plan" for the city. The Olmsteds envisioned a pleasure boulevard following the West Hills that offered great views of the city below, and the city implemented this idea. Unfortunately, the trees that were planted a century ago have grown tall, blocking much of the views and creating a shady park. The street has bike lanes in both directions, making this a great place to ride, although there are some hills.

Pioneer Square (dw)

Tryon Creek State Park *SW Terwilliger Blvd.* A bit off the beaten path, Tryon Creek State Park is the only state natural area within city limits, and it's worth noting. This park is situated in a valley along Tryon Creek, a stream that flows from Multnomah Village southeastward for five miles to the Willamette River. Fourteen miles of trail meander through the park's forested slopes, including a paved all-abilities access trail, an equestrian trail, and a bike path that parallels Terwilliger Blvd. (If you ever need to get to—shudder—Lake Oswego on bike, this path is gonna be your best bet.) Park headquarters and nature center are located at 11321 SW Terwilliger Blvd. It's difficult to get to by bus; the best option is use the #43/Taylors Ferry bus, get off at Taylors Ferry and Terwilliger in South Burlingame, and walk about a mile south on Terwilliger to get to the north entrance of the park.

Washington Park This park is probably the city's most popular (i.e. touristy). From it, you get some spectacular views of the city. Contained within its boundaries are Hoyt Arboretum, the Japanese Garden, Children's Museum, the world-renowned International Rose Test Gardens, and, for better or worse, the World Forestry Center and Portland Zoo. Only the Rose Garden and Arboretum are free, so be prepared to get out the wallet for the other attractions! Expect two things of this park: large crowds, especially on weekends and doubly-especially in the summer; and your parents wanting to come here when they visit you. One way to access the park is from the MAX line's Zoo Station—this stop is the only underground station in the system—where Zoombomb starts. From downtown by surface streets, the easiest access is on SW Park Place west of SW Vista.

Waterfront Park This linear greenway lies along the west bank of the Willamette River between the Steel and Hawthorne bridges. Ages ago, the waterfront was filled with warehouses that housed freight from the ships that plied the river. Around 1940, the commercial buildings on the riverbanks were torn down to make way for Harbor Drive, an ugly monstrosity of a freeway. Downtown was effectively cut off from the river. But not everyone was happy, and in the early 70s, the city tore down the freeway to make room for this park. Progress! Now, you can leisurely stroll the banks of the river and watch the boats go by. During the summer, it seems there's a festival here every week.

The Wildwood Trail This nature trail is a part of the 40-Mile Loop—a trail system in Portland that's actually more than 140-miles long. Roughly 30 miles of the Wildwood Trail goes through Forest Park and Washington Park, and runs along the spine of the West Hills. It begins at the Vietnam Veterans Memorial in Washington Park, heads north through Hoyt Arboretum, passes Pittock Mansion, goes over Balch Creek, and finally terminates at the north end of Forest Park.

The Marquam Trail Lesser known than the longer Wildwood Trail, this 5-mile segment of the 40-Mile Loop connects Terwilliger Parkway to the Wildwood Trail via Council Crest. Unlike the Wildwood, much of this trail winds its way through suburban neighborhoods, and uses on-street routing in some areas. While you're never far from a house or a street while on the Marquam Trail, you're totally immersed in a wooded environment. Because of its accessiblity (MAX station at the north, and Aerial Tram at the south) it's a popular and quick hike for folks. This trail is also part of the 4T Trail network—a loop utilizing Trail, Train (MAX), Tram (Aerial Tram), and Trolley (Portland Streetcar.)

Willamette Park and the West Bank bike path This park (off SW Macadam) is great for river views. If you somehow have a canoe or other watercraft, you could launch it here. There's a paved multi-use path that runs through the park, connecting it to the Sellwood Bridge and the SW Industrial district. This trail is less "natural" than the OMSI/Springwater Trail on the Eastbank because it passes through several apartment and business complexes. In fact, much of the trail is easement over private land. Consequently, there are a lot of sharp turns, so be careful if it's dark and you're on a bicycle!

Director Park *SW Park Ave. at SW Yamhill St.* One of Portland's newest parks, this paved public plaza features an interactive fountain, lots of seating, and underground parking.

Marshall Park *SW 18th Dr. just south of SW Taylors Ferry Road* This shady canyon park contains the upper reaches of Tryon Creek. The small "stepping" waterfall on the west side of the park is my favorite part of Marshall Park!

Plaza Blocks *SW 4th Ave from Jefferson to Salmon* The Plaza Blocks are three separate park blocks located at Portland's "Civic Center": Chapman Square and Lownsdale Square are owned by the city, whereas Terry Schrunk Plaza is owned by the federal government. Chapman and Lownsdale date back to the Civil War era, when the area was the heart of the city and the Park Blocks four blocks farther west were considered "the boonies." In the Victorian era, these two blocks were segregated by gender: Chapman was for the use of women and children, while Lownsdale was "the gentlemen's gathering place." Nowadays, anyone can use either park. However, there's one remnant of the bygone days: Chapman only has a women's restroom and Lownsdale only has a men's! These Park Blocks were also where Occupy Portland camped out in 2011–2012. Schrunk Plaza is newer, built in the 1970s by the federal government for the adjoining Edith Green–Wendall Wyatt Federal Building. (There's underground parking for the feds here.)

This park is named for Portland's longest serving mayor Terry Schrunk, who was in office from 1957 to 1973.

Northwest

Forest Park *NW 29th and Upshur to Newberry Rd.* A 5,000-acre nature preserve located in the hills (Tualatin Mountains) of Northwest Portland, Forest Park is possibly America's largest, forested, urban greenspace. Over 70 miles of trails and firelanes guarantee that you can spend days here exploring the wonders of the outdoors. While all the paths are hikable (including a handicap-accessible trail at the Lower Macleay Trailhead at 2960 NW Upshur), only the Leif Erickson Trail, along with a handful of firelanes, are open to cyclists, much to the chagrin of the local mountain-biking community. (Widish-tired bikes are best suited for the open trails.) Forest Park is one of those places where, once you're in it and surrounded by towering Doug firs, you'll say to yourself, "I can't believe I'm still in a city!" (And dude, you are!) If there's a "Top Ten Reasons Why To Live in Portland" list, I'm sure Forest Park would be on it. There are several ways to enter the park, but the easier options are either via the Wildwood Trail (see separate entry), the Leif Erickson Trailhead at NW Thurman St. west of NW 31st Ave., or the Balch Creek Trailhead at NW Upshur St. and NW 28th Ave.

Pittock Mansion and Park 3229 *NW Pittock Dr. off Burnside* 503-823-3623 A big, fancy-ass house built by former *The Oregonian* publisher Henry L. Pittock back in the early 20th century. Now, it's part of our wonderful park system. Tours are given at the mansion daily (which cost money), if you're into that. If not, come up here to check out the great views of the city and beyond (c'mon, what eccentric millionaire wouldn't build his "castle" on a hill that has one of the best viewpoints in the city, right?), and bring a

(dm)

picnic lunch with you. Bicyclists take note: there are many steep hills to go up in order to get here!

Jamison Square NW 11th Ave. at NW Johnson St. Jamison Square, named after a prominent Pearl District booster, is the first of three new parks built between 2000–2015 in the Pearl District. This park's big selling point is its interactive fountain, which is a very popular place for kids on a hot summer day.

Tanner Springs Park NW 10th Ave. at Marshall St. The second of the three new Pearl District parks. Named after Tanner Creek, the now-covered stream that flowed from the West Hills near Goose Hollow down to the Willamette River (and whose waters Henry Weinhard used for beer brewing.) This park is supposed to replicate the wetlands that used to occupy this area before the expansion of the city. The centerpiece of Tanner Springs Park is its pond and wetlands. While manmade and contrived, the hope is that the wetlands will "do their own thing" and become more "natural."

The Fields Park NW 10th Ave. at Overton St. The last of the three new Pearl District Parks. As it name implies, the Fields Park's primary feature is a big field, which offers a good view of the Fremont Bridge, the crumbling Centennial Mills, the ever-expanding Pearl District, and the railroad tracks (peep an Amtrak train!) There's also an off-leash area for dog that's fenced in.

Wallace Park NW 25th Ave. at Raleigh St. This neighborhood park is fairly standard as neighborhood parks go (though there is an open-to-all play area), but once a year, this park becomes magical! Adjoining Wallace Park is Chapman School. Every September, thousands of small migratory birds called Vaux's Swifts pass through Portland on their way south for the winter. They occupy the chimney at Chapman School because it's a cavernous space that's ideal for sleeping (and because it's the only viable roosting place in this area now that forest space is limited, and dead, hollow trees are in low supply). Just before sunset, anywhere between 1,500 to 35,000 of these birds enter the chimney in an extraordinary display of nature. (And don't worry, this chimney has not been in use since the Swifts started roosting in it about 25 years ago.) So through September, this is "the best show in town," and you can find hundreds to thousands of Portlanders showing up every night to picnic and watch the spectacle. (And if you've read this far and think that I'm joking about this—that this is our version of a snipe hunt and a way to dupe unsuspecting out-of-towners—I assure you, I'm being truthful. Look it up. Besides, there's plenty of things to laugh at like when you mispronounce "Willamette" and when you ask us where the rain is in the summer.)

Pizza

Atlas Pizza *3570 SE Division St. 503-232-3004 AtlasPizzapdx.com* Y'know, with all the new fancy shit opening on the "new" Division St., it's refreshing that a place like this has also opened! Atlas serves up a good, unpretentious pizza, and does it by the slice as well. I dig all the old band posters too.

Pizza-A-Go-Go *3240 N Williams Ave. 503-335-0300 PizzAGo-Go.com* Don't let the cutesy name deceive you; they make a decent pizza! Co-owned by the owner of Bella Faccia, this joint makes a plethora of pies, all in the East-Coast vein. For to-go slices, there's always cheese, pepperoni, a meat combo, veggie combo, and to the delight of many a zinester, a vegan combo (served seven days a week, no less!) They also offer delivery service and salads.

Bella Faccia Pizzeria *2934 NE Alberta St. 503-282-0600 BellaFacciaPizzeria.com* Forget New York, let's talk New Haven! For the uninitiated, the Big Apple is not the only city that takes pride in its pizza. And sure, New Haven-style pizza is quite similar to NY-style, but I think New Havenites take more pride in their product. The generations-running feud between Elm City fixtures Pepe's and Sally's over who makes a better pie is legendary, and known nationwide. Bella Faccia carries the spirit of New Haven pizza to the Alberta Arts District. Firstly, the yardstick for pizza measurement is the cheese slice. You can dress it up as much as you want, but if a pizzeria can't make a good cheese slice, then it can't make pizza. Bella doesn't disappoint there! Secondly, it makes tasty gourmet pies as well. Thirdly, Bella offers damn good vegan slices, loaded with choice veggies and seasoned tempeh on a bean base. Finally, the owner is actually from the New Haven area, so she obviously knows what good pizza is!

Signal Station Pizza *8302 N Lombard St. 503-286-2257 SignalStationPizza.com* Who would have thought it: East Coast pizza in St. Johns, and by the slice, even? Located in an iconic, old filling station, Signal has some pretty tasty pies. And it doesn't hurt that one of the owners is from Connecticut!

Mississippi Pizza *3552 N Mississippi Ave. 503-288-3231 MississippiPizza. com* Long before everything "cool" came about on N Mississippi Ave., there was Mississippi Pizza, offering decent full pies and slices. And they're still around! The adjoining Atlantis Lounge has scads of music shows, and the pizzeria also does gluten-free pies.

Pizza Fino *8225 N Denver Ave. 503-286-2100 Finopdx.com* This Kenton joint is a good go-to for a good New York-style pizza. They also offer other Italian comfort foods, which is hard to come by in this town.

Sizzle Pie *Westside: 624 E Burnside St.; Eastside: 926 W. Burnside St.; Moda Center (Rose Quarter) 1 N Center Court St.; Northeast: 125 NE Schuyler St. 503-234-PIES SizzlePie.com* In 2011, Rocco's Pizza, the long-time punk-rock staple of downtown, shuttered. Its pizza was nothing to write home about. In fact, in our review of the joint we noted that after eating a slice, you'd spend hours mindlessly digesting it. (Some folks somehow thought that was an endorsement.) But the spirit of the place was something else, as it was the refuge of the punk kids, and the starting point for Zoobomb. We all worried that the space at SW 10th and Burnside would become a Gap or something hideous like that. Thankfully, Sizzle Pie came in instead. A bit more "metal" than punk rock, it still fits the vibe. And yes, Virginia, the pizza is loads better than Rocco's could ever manage! Sizzle Pie typically has six to nine by-the-slice options available, all in the East Coast vein: one third veggie, one third meat, and one third vegan options, all the time! Not only that, but the two Burnside locations are open late, so they're the perfect places to hit up after the show to feed your hunger. Delivery available.

American Dream Pizza *4620 NE Glisan St. 503-230-0699 AmericanDreamPizzapdx.com* Portland's old-school, West Coast pizza joint that's been going strong since 1985. Decent pies, good beer selection, plus a load of great pizza-box art on the wall!

East Glisan Pizza Lounge *8001 NE Glisan St 503-279-4273 EastGlisan.com* Newish Montavilla joint that offers up a damn-tasty, East Coast pie, including a great vegan sausage pie! Slices are only offered during two Happy Hours: the earlier (4–6 PM) features a Slice of the Day (meat or veggie) at $2 each; the later (10 PM–midnight) offers a cheese slice for the measely price of $1! The slices aren't that large, but at that price, getting two or three won't break the bank!

Straight from NY *Belmont: 3330 SE Belmont St. 971-279-5970; West: 2241 W Burnside St. 503-228-5260 SFNYpizza.com* A good New York-style joint, hence the name. There are always vegan slices available! The best deal is the four-dollar special: a slice of cheese and a beer (either a tall boy of a watery domestic or a 10-ounce glass of a good microbrew). Add a breadstick and you've got a meal here for under six dollars! Gluten-free pies available.

Baby Doll Pizza *2835 SE Stark St. 503-459-4450 BabyDollPizza.com* A great East Coast pizza joint in the space of the old Stark Naked Pizza. Their regular slices are good, but of note is their Sicilian pies, which is typically offered by the slice. Other places think that "Sicilian-style" means just make the crust thicker, but Baby Doll goes the extra mile and makes that truly airy Sicilian crust.

Escape from New York Pizzeria *622 NW 23rd Ave. 503-227-5423 EFNYpizza.net* Portland's original "pizza by the slice" joint. It's been around since the 1980's. Usually, when a pizzeria bills itself "New York-style," it's overdecorated with Big Apple paraphernalia (for "authenticity") to hide the fact that it has no effing clue what "New York-style" is. While Escape has the NYC décor in spades, don't let that fool you. The pizza chefs here know their shit (excuse my french). The crust is of perfect thickness, and there's the correct balance of sauce and cheese. If you want a slice, there are only three choices: cheese, pepperoni, and the Chef's Special. If you're into gourmet pizza with fancy ingredients, try Pizzicato or Hot Lips. But if you want great pizza from an establishment owned by real New Yorkers, then come here! Tip: Bring your East Coast pals here if they constantly moan, "there's no good pizza on the West Coast."

Flying Pie Pizzeria *7804 SE Stark St. 503-254-2016 Flying-Pie.com* While East Coast Style pizza is definitely my thing, I have developed a taste for some of Portland's older West Coast-style joints. Flying Pie feels worn in, but in the good old-school pizza parlor type of way. Yes, pizza parlor, the type of place that coach would take the little league after a game on Saturday. Red vinyl benches and sports memorabilia on the walls. Pizza parlor! If you show up between 11 AM–3 PM on weekdays, you can order a huge-arsed slice topped your way. If you are of the vegan persuasion, that means you can

Mississippi Records (nb)

order it sans fromage, or if you dare, get soy cheese on it! And don't forget the bread sticks.

Record & Video Stores

North

Mississippi Records 5202 N Albina Ave. 503-282-2990 A dense and well-stocked lil' gem of a record store. Well-priced and often hard-to-find vinyl, as well as cassettes and CDs. Listening stations and friendly staff.

Southeast

Clinton Street Record & Stereo 2510 SE Clinton St. at SE 26th 503-235-5323 ClintonStreetRecordandStereo.com It's located in the spot that once housed record/zine shop Q is for Choir (R.I.P.). An expansion store of the finished selections from Mississippi Records, an electric flavor of all genres, and surprising scores. Plus, stereos!

Discourage Records 1737 SE Morrison St. 503-528-1098 DiscourageRecords.com A record collector's paradise. This store is the place to search for that punk record that has alluded you for years. (Maybe you can find it in pink vinyl?)

Exiled Records 4628 SE Hawthorne Blvd. 503-232-0751 ExiledRecords.com For the consumer who wants rare or avant garde music without the hipster attitude.

Jackpot Records 3574 SE Hawthorne Blvd. 503-239-7561 JackpotRecords.com Probably Portland's most infamous, indie record store, with a large vinyl selection.

Music Millennium 3158 E Burnside St. 503-231-8926 MusicMillennium.com One of the largest independent record retailers in the U.S., and serving Portland since 1969. It's been host to in-store shows with the likes of Paul Westerberg and Joe Strummer (R.I.P.). Bob Mould's video for "I Don't Know You Anymore," off of his 2014 release *Beauty and Ruin,* was shot here. (Hüsker Dü, man!)

Clinton St. Video 2501 SE Clinton St. 503-236-9030 Great selection of cult, indie, and foreign films.

Movie Madness and More 4320 SE Belmont St. 503-234-4363 MovieMadnessVideo.com Huge amount of videos and DVDs for your viewing pleasure. Specializing in the hard to find (documentary, foreign, cult and animation), but also has a good selection of mainstream. And the store is like a mini movie museum, with memorabilia from movies past and present filling the place. There's also something refreshing about the makeshiftness and collageesqueness of the store—a nice change if you're used to the stiflingly-boring, mainstream, movie-rental places. (Do those exist anymore?)

Southwest

2nd Ave. Records *400 SW 2nd Ave. 503-222-3783 2ndAvenueRecords. com* Hidden away in a crevice of downtown, the emphasis here is on new and used hip-hop and punk, t-shirts, and a supposedly good selection of ska.

Restaurants & Other Food Establishments

North

Gravy *3957 N Mississippi Ave. 503-287-8800* Portland is notorious for having bad restaurant service, but Gravy began to change this trend. Great (and huge) tofu and egg dishes, cool flavor combinations, great biscuits, a full bar, and friendly staff. Parents friendly.

Monsoon Thai *4236 N Mississippi Ave. 503-280-7087* Deceptively delicious Thai establishment tucked in the old Soup and Soap building on the corner of Skidmore and Mississippi. (Deceptive in that: they have an awful clipart Italian chef on the cover of their menu, play softrock hits that make your stomach turn, and decorate the place like your mom's pantry.)

Monsoon Thai (nb)

The most important thig about Monsoon is the food—it's genuinely Thai. Moderately priced, like most PDX Thai places, and consistently delicious.

El Burrito Azteca *1942 N Rosa Parks Way 503-841-6667* King Burrito may be the best tacqueria in North Portland. Or maybe it's that place in St. Johns in the back of the mercado? Well, I think Azteca is the best! And its prices are quite reasonable. Pro tip: The adjoining bar is also owned by Azteca, and the food comes from the main kitchen. So if the line in the tacqueria is too long, go to the bar and order a burrito and a beer. You'll get served before those other people in the main line! (Ha! Suckers.) And because the kitchen stays open as late as the bar, Azteca is one of the best late-night burrito options in town.

Proper Eats *8638 N Lombard St. 503-445-2007 ProperEats.wordpress.com* This place is the vegan-cafe outpost of St Johns, and reminds us of those granola places in college towns everywhere. It offers a good selection of food, and you can never go wrong with their tempeh Reuben. Many tasty beers on tap, plus desserts. Worth making the trek all the way up here!

Javier's Taco Shop #2 *121 N Lombard St. 503-286-3186* Javier's is the Rush of Portland tacquerias—that is, people either really like it or really don't. But it's open 24 hours, which is a rarity in this town. So, you know you can always come here!

Tulip Baker (sg)

Tulip Bakery 8322 N Lombard St. 503-286-3444 Owned and operated by the same family for over 60 years, the Tulip is a classic, old-fashion bakery. Go early for fresh bread and donuts, and come here in the late afternoon for cookies hot out of the oven. Respectable selection of cheap and tasty day-olds. Totally worth the trip from any other point in the city!

Northeast

Tonallis Doughnuts & Cream 2805 NE Alberta St. 503-284-4510 In Portland's donutverse, Voodoo reigns as king supreme. It's a shame that Tonallis gets forgotten, because the donuts are really great. And if it's summertime, it offers the ice cream to get you through the hot days. Sure, it's not as hip as Voodoo, but the interior has that authentic donut-shop feel.

Back to Eden Bakery 2217 NE Alberta St. 503-477-5022 Deluxe gluten-free vegan desserts as wild and delicious as your heart can imagine. From pumpkin whoopie pie to strawberry donuts to sundaes to pastries to breakfast items and soups. Vegan soft serve and Coconut Bliss ice cream are available here.

Cup & Saucer 3000 NE Killingsworth St. 503-287-4427 Vegan- and vegetarian-friendly diner fare. Breakfast all day. Also has locations in Kenton on N Denver, and on SE Hawthorne.

Don Pancho Taqueria 2000 NE Alberta St. 503-459-4247 Super-cheap place offering vegan, vegetarian, and meat-tastic food with homemade flare. Very friendly folks. A welcome alternative to the ol' standbys up the street (La Bonita and La Serenita).

Halo Thai 1625 NE Alberta St. 503-546-7063 Family-run Thai restaurant, featuring handcrafted curries and a tasty Pad Thai. I find myself wishing the meals here were simpler and more vibrantly fresh, as I think Thai food should be, but the presentation is done well (both food and atmosphere), and sometimes the taste of the food matches up.

El Nutri Taco 2124 NE Alberta St. 503-473-8447 ElNutriTacopdx.com Vegan Mexican food that feels authentic. Offers soyrizo, moist tortillas, and plentiful avocado. Try the chipotle tempeh burrito.

Paulsen's United Drugs 4246 NE Sandy Blvd. 503-287-1163 This pharmacy has been around since 1918, clearly making it "old school." And what better way to show off its old schoolness than by still having a working soda fountain? Come in to get an ice cream soda or cherry phosphate, and enjoy the free Wi-Fi service.

La Serenita 2817 NE Alberta St. 503-335-8283 One of Portland's most popular Mexican taquerias. Rumors swing both ways about the presence of lard in the beans. It used to host punk shows here. Also has a location in Sellwood.

La Bonita *2839 NE Alberta 503-281-3662 LaBonitaRestaurant.net* Decent, authentic Mexican tacquria, and veggie-friendly too. Also has a location on N Killingsworth.

The Sudra *2333 NE Glisan St. 971-302-6002 TheSudra.com* Gourmet, Portland-influenced, vegan Indian food. Offers soy curls, kale salad with homemade dressing, chutneys, and pickled anaheims.

Vita Café *3023 NE Alberta St. 503-335-8233 Vita-Cafe.com* Once the sister to The Paradox in SE, Vita Café is one of Portland's older, vegan-friendly restaurants that specializes in comfort food. Come for the vegan fish and chips, chicken-fried steak, and Philly steak sandwiches. Happy Hour is all night on Wednesdays.

Annie's Donuts *3449 NE 72nd Ave. (at Sandy/Fremont) 503-284-2752* One of Portland's good old-school donut shops. Annie's is the ying to Voodoo's yang in Portland's donutverse: Annie's is open during the day, whereas Voodoo is only open at night; Annie's is unpretentious and plain, whereas Voodoo is hip and quirky; Annie's seems to be solely occupied by old men reading newspapers (and if that doesn't speak old-school donut shop, I don't know what does!), while Voodoo has punks and hipsters hanging out there. Try the Butterfly bar, which has chocolate and peanut butter on it. And despite that Annie's has been serving this donut since probably the Eisenhower administration, the staff will always, always ask if you meant a "buttermilk" bar. Nope, gimme the Butterfly! (Sorry, no vegan donuts.)

Fairley's Pharmacy *7206 NE Sandy Blvd. (at Fremont) 503-284-1159 FairleysPharmacy.com* The old-school, independent drugstore—the type that contains a soda fountain and maybe a postal counter—is a very endangered

(sg)

species in not only Portland, but in the world. Many Portlanders fondly fetishised Seaton Pharmacy at SE 60th and Belmont (open transom, anyone?), but that closed, along with the Nob Hill Pharmacy. Both of those places were featured in Gus Van Sant's classic 1989 movie *Drugstore Cowboy*. While Fairley's didn't make that cut, it's one of the very few soda-fountain pharmacies left in town, so if you want to get a Cherry Phosphate, make sure you head here. (No postal counter, as they died off with the closing of Dickson's and Phoenix.)

Southeast

Canteen *2816 SE Stark St. 503-922-1858 Canteenpdx.com* A hipster, deluxe-presentation, vegan juice bar with a solid food menu as well. Taco salads, bowls, smoothies, oatmeal, cheesecakes, and so much more.

Dots *2521 SE Clinton St. at SE 26th 503-235-0203* This neat bar/ restaurant located in the heart of the Clinton neighborhood has a dark ambience and comfy booth seating. The velvet wallpaper and velvet big-eyed children paintings are all the rage with the cool kids. (And since the smoking ban went into effect, you can actually see that wallpaper!) Veggie and vegan options are offered alongside traditional diner fare. Serves food late into the eve.

Los Gorditos Restaurant *1212 SE Division St. 503-445-6289* If someone had only one day to spend in Portland, I would have them eat lunch here. It's an authentic Mexican cart-turned-restaurant that features an all-vegan menu as well as a meat menu. The food is great and it offers soy curls and Daiya cheese on the vegan dishes. It also features art shows

Juniors Café (ng)

with a friendly atmosphere. It's a great place to see black-clad anarchists reading giant academic texts. Not to be missed! Please note: Los Gorditos only accepts cash, so have that ready unless you want to pay the high service fees at the ATM located in restaurant. Also has a "food truck" location at SE 50th just north of Powell, and a restaurant in The Pearl at NW Davis and 10th. The Pearl location does accept credit cards, but the food here costs more than the other locations.

Harlow *3632 SE Hawthorne Blvd. 971-255-0138 HarlowpPdx.com* Come to hear new-age people talk about their relationship problems in public and see the largest collection of yoga pants available anywhere in the city. Stay for the delicious, gluten-free veggie and vegan bowls, elaborate entrees, scrumptious juices and smoothies, deluxe and interesting side dishes, delicious BBQ tempeh, and lots and lots of vegetables.

Junior's *1742 SE 12th Ave. 503-467-4971* Breakfast and lunch establishment started by the people at Dots. Great breakfast fare and vegan friendly.

Laughing Planet *3320 SE Belmont St. 503-235-6472 LaughingPlanetCafe. com* The cooks here make a fine n' dandy bean and cheese burrito, but Laughing Planet excels in the art of making "fancy burritos," using feta cheese, broccoli, jicama, and even cactus and SPAM! Tofu, soy cheese, and vegan sour cream are also available. So yeah, it's not "authentica," but there are other places in town you can go to for that. While you're here, check out all the R. Crumb reproductions

Paradox Café (nb)

on the wall. There are also many other Laughing Planet locations scattered throughout the city.

Nicholas' Restaurant *318 SE Grand Ave. 503-235-5123 NicholasRestaurant.com* Traditional and delicious Mediterranean fare. Vegan mezza option. And vegan baklava (if you don't mind honey)! Tiny, very popular, and tends to fill up fast, so come early. Or go to the newer location on NE Broadway, which usually doesn't have a wait. Or, even better, ride the Springwater Corridor all the way out to Gresham and eat at the downtown location there!

Paradox *3439 SE Belmont at SE 35th 503-232-7508 ParadoxOrganicCafe. com* The old-school vegan/vegetarian standby. The Paradox specializes in inexpensive meatless meals, though it does offer a meat hamburger (cooked on a separate grill), hence the paradox. Breakfast is served all day! The hours of operation have been reduced to breakfast and lunch hours, so no more late-night pie runs here.

Northwest

Mio Sushi *2271 NW Johnson St. 503-221-1469 MioSushi.com* Relatively cheap sushi in an unpretentious atmosphere. Good veggie menu. Happy Hour is Monday through Friday from 4 PM through 6 PM.

Pearl Bakery *102 NW 9th Ave. 503-827-0910 PearlBakery.com* Sweet-ass sweets that you will dig, yo. You can't go wrong with their dessert treats. Features "artisan" breads.

Sisters of the Road Café *133 NW 6th Ave. 503-222-5694 SistersoftheRoad. org* Super cheap café, designed to serve low-income folks, where you can work in exchange for food.

Skateboarding

by Jered Bogli

One might think that given Oregon's rainy climate the skateboard scene would be as soggy as the weather. In fact, the skate scene is one of the most vibrant in the country. Oregon and the rest of the Northwest has become the epicenter for the new skatepark-building revolution. The DIY-ethic of the Burnside Skatepark served to launch this movement and give rise to a few companies dedicated to excellent concrete skateparks. Currently in Portland, we have laws in place that give skateboarding the same treatment any other mode of transportation. What that means exactly is a little foggy. In part, it means skateboarders have to obey the same traffic laws as motorists do. It also means you can skate all over downtown. However, many spots are a bust, and despite skating being legal, you could say the legality of skating ends as soon as your wheels come off the ground. Locally, there are a couple of skateparks located close to downtown, as well as countless others in the suburbs. Street spots tend to come and go quickly. The six months of rain, and the use of studded tires, makes for some rough streets. Skating for transportation can be frustrating unless you have some big, soft, cruiser wheels. Luckily, the relatively small size of Portland, combined with the usually temperate summer weather and a first-class bus and rail system, actually makes getting around the city on your board enjoyable and fairly efficient.

If you're looking for some new stuntwood while in town, there are a number of shops to choose from depending on your aesthetic. (Ah, the fashion of skateboarding.) Close to downtown, there are two major core skateshops. First off, you have Cal Skate, located at 210 NW 6th Ave. (*503-248-0495, Monday–Friday, 11 AM–6 PM, Saturday 10 AM–6 PM, Suunday 11 AM–5 PM, calsk8.com*) The inside of Cal Skate is a veritable skate museum, old decks and skate ephemera lining all the walls. This shop is an institution here in town. Much goodness comes out of the shop and its employees have their hands in most of what is happening in the Portland skate scene. This is the only shop of the two that only stocks skate gear—talk about core! Going to the east side of the Willamette River is Cal's Pharmacy (no relation to Cal Skate—don't ask!) at 1400 E Burnside St. (*503-233-1237*). There are more shops in town, but those are the main independent/local players close in.

As for skateparks, under the east side of the Burnside Bridge is the fabled DIY park that shares the same name as the bridge. The cement starting pouring over 25 years ago and this park continues to evolve thanks to the love and devotion of many of the original builders and new recruits. Burnside has a reputation for being a rough place; however, if you employ a bit of common sense, you'll find that Burnside is quite friendly—a bit like a surly, old grandfather or something. Learning how to skate Burnside is a lifelong process, so be forewarned. Some of the best times to show up and have a mellow session would be in the early morning (although not allowed in the park, BMX kids are usually there early morning). There also tends to be a lull in the action around 10:30 AM–12:30 PM, so you're fine to learn a few lines then. Once the hardcore locals start showing up, it's best to find a good vantage point and watch the madness ensue. If you've got common sense, you'll know when your time is up, and when to sit back, watch and try to memorize a couple new lines for the next time. If you skate, you must experience Burnside.

Commonwealth (*1425 SE 20th Ave.*) is a small indoor spot, and an interesting one because it's concrete. The bowl is small, but an interesting shape and make. There's a small street area as well. Overall, it's a fun spot and a great option for wet days.

Holly Farm (*10819 SW Capitol Hwy.*) is deep in SW Portland and is an odd little park—more of a "skate spot" than a skatepark. Depending, the park centers around a round-ish bowl with a spine in the middle.

Gabriel Park (*SW Vermont St.*) is a very fun park, and it's more or less modeled on a classic snakerun—some fun hips, rollers and a high to low setup that makes keeping your speed up a fun challenge. Gabriel has one deep wall and a mellow shallow area as well. Overall Gabriel is a great place to spend a morning rolling around.

Outer NE Portland is chock full of skateparks these days. Glenhaven (*2735 NE 82nd Ave.*) was the first skatepark built and is mostly a street park; however, there's a six-foot bowl that has some interesting lines, and a pool complete with steps and proper pool coping. The street area is super fun and very skateable, with faux brick banks, quaterpipes, and a wall that seems to be like the old Berkley tennis courts—good luck. This all centers around a rollin/step up and hip, so the crash-up derby factor can be high when the park is crowded; the pool and bowl are usually empty. Lots of scooter kids and BMX bikes here.

Ed Benedict (*out past I-205 on Powell Blvd.*) is a full-on street plaza with ledges, rails, gaps...you name it. If you want a street spot, this is the place to go. Not much in way of services close by, so you best show up with some water and snacks if you're planning on a longer session. Super smooth and good flow overall.

Most recently built is Khunamokwst (Cully) Skatepark (*5225 NE Alberta St.*). This is also a "skate spot." The bowl is tiny and everytime I skate it I am afraid I'll break an ankle. If you have some skills there are ample fun lines to be had. Likewise, if you're less confident, this is a great spot to just roll around and get your legs back under you.

Way up in North Portland by the transit center in Pier Park (*N. Seneca and St. Johns, off of N Lombard St.*) is the St. Johns Skatepark. This park is mostly bowls, a tiny beginner bowl, and a midsize bowl that, despite being mostly six-feet deep, has very quick transitions and is hard to skate with confidence. There's also a deep bowl which I believe is 12.5-feet deep: all pool coping and tile. Connected to the deep bowl is a giant full pipe with a "mouse hole" roll in—super fun and super fast. Also, there's a small street section to the park as well.

If you have access to a car, Newberg (*1201 S Blaine St. in Newberg, OR*) is a must. Newberg has been called the "best skatepark in the world" by more than one person, plus Newberg is the birthplace of Herbert Hoover. The park is 28,000 sq. ft. of perfectly poured concrete. It must be experienced to be believed. The park ranges in size from three feet to 12 feet, and features a great vert capsule/elbow combo, snake runs, and more lines than one person could ever skate. The only thing you need is a helmet—the rule is enforced (though not so much lately, so you could get by without a helmet now). The park has shady picnic tables, water fountains, and porta-potties. Behind the vert section of the park is a river that's a good place to cool off in the summer. The park is open from sunrise to dark.

If you're into backyard style pools and you've made it to Newberg, you should then head to Donald (*10853 Donald Rd. NE in Aurora, OR*) to skate the pool there, complete with steps in the shallow end. An addition to the park is a fun mini half with a pump bump in the middle and bowl corners on one side.

The options for skateparks are endless if you have a car. You could make a day out of Hood River and Bingen. Vancouver, WA has a few good parks, as well as Battleground, WA. If you have a full day, Lincoln City Oregon is pretty much heaven. The whole Oregon coast is littered with skateparks. Eugene, OR just finished an amazing new park. Windells Snowboard Camp has an epic skatepark, depending on the time of year it offers public sessions on the weekend. You could easily make a month out of Oregon and Washington and never skate the same park twice.

NorthwestSkater.com
SkateOregon.com
Sleestak.net

Theaters

Portland is a great town to see a movie in. Sure, we've got our share of corporate owned multiplexes, and an IMAX even. But what makes Portland moviegoing special is the sheer number of independent neighborhood theaters—most of them were built from the teens to the 1930s when movie theaters were very big deals— that are still running! And many of these theaters serve beer and pizza!

North

St. Johns Twin Cinemas *8704 N Lombard St. 503-286-1768 StJohnsCinema.com* Opened in 1913, this Spanish-style theater was also known as the Northgate. Its two screens show first-run movies. Beer and pizza are served.

St. Johns Theater and Pub *8203 N Ivanhoe St. 503-283-8520 McMenamins.com/StJohns* Not to be confused with the nearby St. Johns Twin, this theater currently occupies the building that was built in 1905 for the Lewis and Clark Exposition—Portland's "World Fair". The domed structure was used for the National Cash Register Company's exhibit hall. After the Expo, it was barged down the Willamette River to its current location in St. Johns, and it's one of the few things to survive that fair! McMenamins staples can be found here: beer, food, and second-run movies.

Northeast

Hollywood Theatre *4122 NE Sandy Blvd. 503-281-4215 HollywoodTheatre. org* Built by architects John Virginius Bennes and Harry A. Herzog in the Spanish Colonial Revival Style, the 1,500-seat Hollywood opened its doors on July 17, 1926 with the film *More Pay–Less Work*. The Hollywood was, and still is, one of the most ornate movie palaces in the Pacific Northwest, built in a time when theaters were meant to stand out. With its uniquely beautiful facade, the theater quickly became a fixture in the neighborhood,

Hollywood Theatre (lg)

Movie

so much so that the commercial district along Sandy Blvd. surrounding the Hollywood Theatre was named after it (not the other way around!). This is the only time in Portland history when a neighborhood has been named after a building. Like the Bagdad Theater in SE, the Hollywood started as a cinema/vaudeville house, but switched to just showing movies sometime mid-century. The Hollywood got into the widescreen game when it became Cinerama-capable in the early 1960s. In 1975, to better compete with the cineplex competition, its balcony was converted into two smaller auditorums—a setup that remains to this day. Sadly, the Hollywood went through its slump years from the late 1970s through to the early 1990s. The turnaround came in April of 1997, when the Oregon Film & Video Foundation bought the ailing cinema. Committed to restoring the Hollywood Theatre to its original luster, its new owners have been extensively renovating the theater inside and out, including replacing the marquee and relighting the main sign. Currently, the Hollywood shows an eclectic mix of international, indie/arthouse, and local films, as well as hosting various film festivals. And it's one of the few places that can show films in 70 mm format!

Kennedy School *5736 NE 33rd Ave. 503-249-3983 McMenamins. com/427-Kennedy-School-home* Originally an elemetary school when it opened in 1915 (and closed due to disrepair in 1980), Kennedy School was renovated by McMenamins, and it's now an arty neighborhood hub with a restaurant, three specialty bars, lodging ($$!), hot tubs, a brewhouse, gym, and theater. Most locals know it for the budget theater/pub with old couches and easy chairs. The building is fun to explore with lots of creepy art.

(sg)

Laurelhurst Theater 2735 E Burnside St. 503-232-5511 *LaurelhurstTheater.com* Built in 1923, the Laurelhurst was one of the first art-deco styled buildings to grace the City of Roses. It served as a neighborhood cinema throughout the years, but the Cineplex era brought upon the Laurelhurst hard times. The Laurelhurst tried everything possible to stay afloat. In 1979, the theater was divided into four, smaller screening rooms (the current format here today) to compete with the cineplexes, but it didn't do much. During the 80s and 90s, the Laurelhurst adopted a cheap-ticket, B-movie and second-run format and earned the nickname "The Urine-Hurst" due to the state of its clientele (and surrounding neighborhood). Around 2000, the theater was bought and renovated by its current owners. With a renewed sense of respect, the Laurelhurst Theater has become a community hub again for the surrounding Kerns/Buckman neighborhood and the jumpin' commercial district along 28th Ave. It offers beer and pizza!

Roseway Theater 7229 NE Sandy Blvd. 503-282-2733; Showtimes: 503-282-2898 *RosewayTheater.com* Built in 1924 and opened in 1925, the single-screen Roseway has been in continuous operation for over 90 years. Passing through many hands over the years, this theater almost closed for good in the 90s. In 1999, the Kane siblings bought the Roseway, determined to return it to its original luster. The Roseway is one of the few independent theaters in the city that still shows first-run Hollywood fare. Its well preserved Art Deco interior and exterior makes the Roseway a landmark in this district.

granton ∧ 6/04

Roseway Theatre (sg)

Southeast

Academy Theater 7818 SE Stark St. 503-252-0500 *AcademyTheaterpdx. com* Originally opened in 1948, the Academy served as the neighborhood theater of Montavilla until it shuttered in the 1970s. The space was used for less glamorous things until 2006, when the Academy was brought back to life. Restored to its 1948 glory, the Academy Theater beams with late Deco Era energy. The three screens show a good selection of second-run fare, and beer and pizza from neighboring Flying Pie are available. For families, the theater provides day care for early showings!

Avalon/Wunderland 3451 SE Belmont St. 503-238-1617 *WunderlandGames.com* Portland's nickel arcade, and also a great place to see cheap second-run movies.

Bagdad Theatre and Pub 3702 SE Hawthorne Blvd. 503-467-7521; Movie line: 503-249-7474 *McMenamins.com* Ah, what's not to like about the Bagdad? It's been a landmark on Hawthorne Blvd. for three-quarters of a century, and has always been a focal point and source of pride for the neighborhood. Universal Pictures built the Bagdad in 1927, spending the then-enormous sum of $100,000 for this opulent movie and vaudeville palace. It's Middle-Eastern meets California Deco architecture was appealing then as it is now. It retained its live vaudeville productions through the 1940s, and then converted to its current all-movie format. In 1974, the original backstage area was converted into a screening room called, cleverly enough, the Backstage, which showed mostly B-movies. In 1975, the Bagdad was the chosen theater for the Oregon premiere of *One Flew Over the Cuckoo's Nest*, the movie based off of Oregon-native Ken Kesey's novel. Actors Jack Nicholson and Louise Fletcher, and producer Michael Douglas were all on hand. In 1979, it was converted into a tri-plex after having trudged through the mid-century with its one-screen format. In 1991, the theater was purchased by those ever-enterprising McMenamin brothers, who renovated the "grand dame of Hawthorne" and made it the brewpub and first-run movie theater we currently know and love. During its renovation period in 1991, the Bagdad saw yet another Hollywood premiere: *My Own Private Idaho*, the feature directed by Portlander Gus Van Sant and starring River Phoenix (R.I.P.) and Keanu Reaves.

Cinemagic 2021 SE Hawthorne Blvd. 503-231-7919 *TheCinemagicTheater. com* An eclectic mix of arty and second-run films at this long-standing movie house (100 years old, and with many names over the years.) Now serving beer! Cheaper movies on Tuesdays.

Clinton St. Theater 2522 SE Clinton St. 503-238-5588 *CSTpdx.com* Opened in 1915, the Clinton is one of the oldest continuously running theaters in Portland. This theater has had the *Rocky Horror Picture Show* playing every Saturday night for over 30 years! During its lifetime, the Clinton has been called many things. Originally the Clinton, its name changed to the less-distinctive 26th Avenue Theatre in 1945, and then to the not-much-better Encore in 1969. Finally in 1976, it reverted back to the name we know and love. The Clinton is known for showing arthouse and indie films, and for having interestingly-themed movie fests, like Stag Film Festival, Hump, and, most notably, Dog Day (a film fest that invited dogs in the theater to watch movies like *Rin Tin Tin*, among others!)

(sg)

Moreland Theatre *6712 SE Milwaukie Ave. (near Bybee Blvd) 503-236-5257 MorelandTheater.com* Opened in 1926, the Moreland has been in continuous operation since then, keeping the same name for its over 90 year history. The Moreland is special because it still has a single screen and it still shows first-run Hollywood films (versus second-run or arthouse fare that many of the historic theaters in town offer). The interior and exterior have been preserved, retaining the look and feel of a Deco Era cinema.

Southwest

Living Room Theaters *341 SW 10th Ave. 971-222-2010 LivingRoomTheaters.com* Upscale six-screen cinema showing arty/indie films in smaller theaters with recliners instead of traditional movie seats (hence the "living room"). Unlike other cinemas, food and drinks are actually delivered to you!

(ks)

Northwest

Cinema 21 616 NW 21st Ave. 503-223-4515 Cinema21.com The Northwest neighborhood's independently-owned, first-run, arthouse theater. Regularly shows indie flicks you won't find elsewhere. Also hosts a number of film festivals.

Mission Theater and Pub 1624 NW Glisan St. 503-223-4527 McMenamins.com Talk about history! Way back in the early 1890s, what is now the Mission Theater was a church for the Swedish Evangelical Mission, a place where missionaries planned pilgrimages to Asia. Eventually, the church moved on, and the Mission became a Longshoreman's Hall. In 1987, McMenamins renovated the space, and it now offers cheap movies and beer! Viva cheap movies!

Useful Resources

Northeast

Dignity Village *9325 NE Sunderland Ave. (off of NE 33rd Ave. near NE Marine Drive)* In December 2000, a group of homeless individuals decided to do something to get themselves out of the doorways. They set up five tents on public land, and Dignity Village was born. Through hard work, determination, public support, and resourcefulness, Dignity Village has grown and thrived to be a self-governing village that houses formerly homeless people, and with the city's approval. The residents build their own shelters and take part in the Village's decisions. It's currently in the process of moving on to a new phase by establishing a perma-site based on their on-going model. In its current location, Dignity Village makes use of environmentally-friendly materials such as strawbale, and uses wind-generated electricity. Dignity Village serves as a unique model of one effective solution for homelessness, and is one of the oldest on-going homeless villages in the country. It has gained interest from homeless advocates from around the world. Visitors are welcome to drop by.

Southeast

Independent Publishing Resource Center (IPRC) *1001 SE Division St.* 503-827-0249 IPRC.org The IPRC facilitates creative expression and identity by providing individuals access to the resources

IPRC (ar)

and tools for the creation of independently published media and art. It's a nonprofit resource center that features a zine lending library (with library cards available to all), zine workspace and supplies, and a computer lab. Other things available are a copier, book-binding supplies, letterpresses, a mimeograph machine, art gallery, and more. Workshops on various aspects of independent publishing and DIY art are available. The IPRC is open to members and to non-members (for a small hourly fee). No zine-related visit to Portland is complete without hitting up the IPRC!

FREE GEEK *1731 SE 10th Ave. 503-232-9350 FREEGEEK.org* The lifespan of the average new computer these days is measured in months, not years. The vast majority of these "old," unwanted computers end up in landfills or are shipped overseas, where the parts poison the people and the land. FREE GEEK is a non-profit that aims to stop this while arming underprivileged folks with computers. The staff collects, assesses, reuses, and recycles computer hardware that individuals and organizations donate to them. The hardware is sorted and tested by volunteers who help the cause, and learn about computers at the same time. All parts that can be reused are used, and those that can't are responsibly sold as scrap or recycled. In the end, the volunteers get their own computer for their efforts, which they conveniently learned all about during the process! Additionally, FREE GEEK has classes, all sorts of outreach programs, sells or donates hardware to nonprofits, and has a thrift store open to the public. Plus so much more!

Southwest
Outside In *1132 SW 13th Ave. 503-535-3800 OutsideIn.org (medical appointments call 503-223-4121)* Outside In is a social-service agency dedicated to serving low-income adults and homeless youth. Current programs include: a community health clinic that provides very low-cost, sliding-scale pay service, a homeless-youth program designed to help homeless youths obtain independent living, and risk education. Outside In is a great place to go

Hawthorne Blvd., looking west from SE 38th
(dw)

if you need non-emergency medical treatment and have no money. The only drawback is you have to be under 30 to use the traditional medical clinic. (Naturopathic doctors and interns, acupuncturists, and Chinese herbalists are available for people of all ages.) Clinic hours are Mon–Fri; see its website or call to find out what its hours are, as it varies daily depending on the service.

Ever-nebulous "Other" Category

Adult Soapbox Derby *Annually in August SoapboxRacer.com* The real life version of your childhood dreams of building (or just watching) the coolest life-size soapbox derby cars racing down Mount Tabor. So much fun!

Benson Bubblers *All around town* So, most cities have public drinking fountains, but only Portland has Benson Bubblers. The bubblers were started by civic leader and wealthy guy Simon Benson in the 'teens. Benson was concerned about all the drunk loggers seen around town, and figured that if there were reliable public sources of drinking water to be found, alcoholism would be curbed. The first bubbler went into place at SW 5th and Washington in 1912, and by 1917, 40 fountains could be found around town. Presently, there are 52 bubblers, most are the classic four-bowl design, but some are only single bowls. Make sure you take a drink from one when you're thirsty!

Blow Pony *BlowPony.com Fourth Saturday of every month (check Facebook page for event info)* This giant, queer, dance party with four DJs will rock your neon socks off. Like a real-life version of the clubs Stefan describes on Saturday Night Live? "You will dance with strangers. You will see people of every imaginable body type wearing anything from... well, nothing, to clown suits, to pony costumes, to dominatrix outfits."

Other

Downtown food carts (dw)

Food Carts! *Everywhere, All the time!* Now that we have over 600 food carts within the city limits (and they're changing faster than Portlanders change their clothes), it's simply impossible to catalog them in this guide. However, please eat at them and experiment and don't let one or two bad experiences deter you from a third or fourth.

Monday Fun Day *Col. Summers Park, 20th and Belmont, Every Monday 12p-10p* Since *Portlandia's* adult hide-and-seek league isn't actually real (or is it?), this will have to do. It's all kinds of fun sports and physical activities in a public park for any adult who wants to join in. A superfun site!

OMSI After Dark *1945 SE Water Ave. 503-797-4000 OMSI.edu/afterdark* What adult wouldn't be excited about hanging out at this giant science museum when alcohol is served and kids are nowhere to be found? Last Friday of the month, typically.

Pecularium *2234 NW Thurman St. 503-227-3164 Peculiarium.com* A museum featuring, among other things, an interactive exhibit that allows you to become the subject of an alien autopsy, and a cool Yeti.! Imagine pairing the scary cases from the X-Files with an ice cream from their counter, and you'll get this place.

Plaid Pantry *Locations scattered all over the Portland Metro area* Our own local 7-11, but with a much cheesier name. (And nothing there is plaid, either!) You're probably near one right now. Specializes in cheap 24-ounce cans of PBR. FYI: Plaid has a "no chase policy," and if you really need a job, you can probably get one there.

Santa Con Ever wanted to go on a pub crawl dressed as Santa Claus with hundreds of other Santas? Yup, me too. Happens in December, obviously. Google it.

The Unipiper *Randomly seen on the street all over town* A man wearing a Darth Vader mask, riding a unicycle, playing the bagpipes, with fire coming out of them. Was Portland cool enough to attract such an individual or is he exactly what makes Portland so cool? This is the question of the Portland millennium.

Portland Urban Iditarod *End of February* This is a fun scavenger hunt if you and your friends like the idea of racing across the city (alcohol-fueled) with a shopping cart.

Woodstock Mystery Hole *"Two miles west of I-205" in the Woodstock neighborhood BarronMind.com/wmh.htm* After the Bretz floods of the Ice Age, layers of hardened rock were buried under sediment. Climb into a hole in the ground that may contain artifacts from an ancient civilization.

Rocky Butte (Joseph Wood Hill) Park
looking east towards Mt. Hood

SUBSCRIBE TO EVERYTHING WE PUBLISH!

Do you love what Microcosm publishes?

Do you want us to publish more great stuff?

Would you like to receive each new title as it's published?

Subscribe as a BFF to our new titles and we'll mail them all to you as they are released!

$10-30/mo, pay what you can afford. Include your t-shirt size and month/date of birthday for a possible surprise! Subscription begins the month after it is purchased.

microcosmpublishing.com/bff

...AND HELP US GROW YOUR SMALL WORLD!